~ THE TRIAL OF JACK THE RIPPER ~

EUAN MACPHERSON

THE TRIAL OF JACK THE RIPPER

THE CASE OF WILLIAM BURY (1859–89)

MAINSTREAM
PUBLISHING
EDINBURGH AND LONDON

First published in Great Britain in 2005 by
MAINSTREAM PUBLISHING COMPANY
(EDINBURGH) LTD
7 Albany Street
Edinburgh EH1 3UG

ISBN 1 84596 011 4

A catalogue record for this book is available
from the British Library

Typeset in Stone

Printed in Great Britain by
William Clowes Ltd, Beccles, Suffolk

ACKNOWLEDGEMENTS

I WOULD LIKE TO OFFER MY WARMEST THANKS TO MARGARET Drummond, who encouraged me to return to this project after an absence of 17 years. I must also thank Richard and Molly Whittington-Egan for their advice, interest and encouragement. Sergeant William McFarlane (Retd) of Tayside Police spent a long time discussing the case with me and showed me around Tayside Police Museum. He was kind enough to leaf through Dundee City Police records from 1889 and came up with a lot of information about the police officers who investigated the case.

Thanks also to Ken Bruce LLB, Dr John Drummond, Alan Hay, Iain Flett (Dundee City Archives), Neil Millar and Tessa Spencer (National Archives of Scotland), Andrew Stewart (Clerk of the Faculty of Advocates), Mike Weir MP and the Local Studies staff at Central Library, Dundee.

CONTENTS

FOREWORD

ALTHOUGH IT IS NOW 117 YEARS SINCE THE WHITECHAPEL KILLER ripped the life from his five pathetic victims, when I was born a mere 36 years had elapsed since the commission of the crimes. And it is possible, probable even, that he, Jack the Ripper, was still alive. But then, after reading Euan Macpherson's conclusions, I thought maybe not!

Ever since I paid, at the age of 11, my first visit to Whitechapel – just in time to catch the fading shades of horror in the eyes of ageing East Enders who had actually witnessed the awful events of 1888 – I have watched for the past 70 years as the long procession of suspects has been – literally – booked.

Although there had been a 32-page, threepenny pamphlet, *The Whitechapel Horrors, Being an Authentic Account of the Jack the Ripper Murders*, published by the Daisy Bank Printing and Publishing Company of Manchester in the 1920s, its author, Tom Robinson, an old-style Fleet Street journalist, beyond reporting that a policeman who had been on the beat at the time always believed that the Ripper was a foreign sailor, hazards no guess as to the identity of the killer.

It all began in earnest – the guessing-game, that is – with Leonard Matters's book, *The Mystery of Jack the Ripper*, which was published in 1929, and his accused was the surely fictitious Dr Stanley.

After that, there was a break until 1937, when a pre-Paperback Revolution paperback, *Jack the Ripper, or, When London Walked in Terror*, issued from the none-too-impressive pen

9

of Edwin T. Woodhall, a retired London detective who, despite introducing George Chapman, aka Severin Klosowski, as one whom 'many believe to have been none other than Jack the Ripper himself', supported Matters's now generally discredited Dr Stanley nomination. A couple of years later, in 1939, William Stewart brought out *Jack the Ripper: A New Theory*, which put Jill the Ripper, a sadistic midwife, in the dock.

A further 20 years were to elapse before Donald McCormick perpetrated a fantasy titled *The Identity of Jack the Ripper*, in which a totally bogus Russian dubbed Dr Alexander Pedachenko was paraded as the indisputable Ripper.

Considerably more plausible – although in my view not guilty – was the suspect brought forward in Tom Cullen's *Autumn of Terror: Jack the Ripper, His Crimes and Times* (1968): Montague John Druitt, barrister and schoolmaster. The involvement of the Royal Family, in the dubious shape of the Duke of Clarence, aided and abetted by the royal physician, Sir William Gull, was heralded in 1976 by Stephen Knight's *Jack the Ripper: The Final Solution*. This is an answer to the riddle which has been widely – though in my opinion wrongly – accepted.

And in 1994 that doughty researcher and professional explorer of myths, the late Melvin Harris, finally declared his belief that Robert D'Onston Stephenson was the culprit. The previous year had seen the absurd nomination of the Liverpool cotton broker James Maybrick as the East End slaughterman, in *The Diary of Jack the Ripper* narrative by Shirley Harrison. I consider Maybrick to be as unlikely a suspect as that other Liverpudlian, the wife-killer James Kelly, who was James Tully's choice for the Ripper in *The Secret Prisoner 1167*.

Stewart Evans and Paul Gainey submitted their own candidate for the bloodstained laurels in *The Lodger: The Arrest and Escape of Jack the Ripper* (1995). He was an American herbalist and medical mountebank, Dr Francis J. Tumblety. So meticulously is their prosecution case fashioned that one hesitates before, eventually, declining to convict. That same year Bruce Paley offered up Joseph Barnett, Mary Jane Kelly's lover, as the guilty party.

Then there is Walter Sickert, indicted first by Jean Overton Fuller in 1990, and again, with a fanfare of brass trumpets, in 2002 by Patricia Cornwell in her somewhat over-confidently titled *Portrait of a Killer: Jack the Ripper – Case Closed*, wherein, incidentally, she contrives never to so much as mention the work of her predecessor in that particular field. Not that it really matters, for neither of them succeeds in making the libel stick.

The foregoing is just a selection of some of the more rationally, or at any rate less *irrationally* based suspects, out of upwards of a hundred widely and indeed wildly nominated candidates.

There is to my mind absolutely no doubt that Mr Macpherson's nominee is deserving of our fullest attention. The 29-year-old Englishman whom he would bring to the bar of justice is a miscreant and murderer by the name of William Henry Bury. This is not strictly Bury's first committal. He was summoned with a case to answer by Mr Macpherson in his article 'Jack the Ripper in Dundee' in the *Scots Magazine* back in January 1988; and thereafter by William Beadle, in his *Jack the Ripper: Anatomy of a Myth* (1995); and by Stewart Evans in an article, 'The Ripper's Nemesis', in the magazine *Rippermania* in January 1997. And there can be no gainsaying that in a great many aspects his circumstances do fit in most satisfyingly with those which could well have applied to Jack the Ripper.

Admittedly, though, it does require a conscious effort of will for those of us who have grown long-toothed in the service of Ripperology, and accustomed to the picture of the dark, wraith-like slayer shadow flitting murderously through the East End night, to readjust to the novel visualisation of a solid, bearded figure set against an alien Caledonian background. Even so . . .

If Jack the Ripper had in fact exhibited surgical skill, this would, Mr Macpherson agrees, have put paid to Bury as a viable suspect, for there is no rhyme or reason, no evidence, to support the notion that he was so endowed. But, equally, there is no secure *evidence* – merely conflicting *opinion* – that 'Jack the Whitechapel knife' wielded it with a practised anatomist's or a surgeon's touch.

Even supposing that you are not prepared to accept – that you resist – the idea of William Henry Bury as the veritable Ripper, Mr Macpherson's book is still of prime value as the first complete account of the misdeeds, investigation, trial and ultimate fate of a man who shows himself a classic practitioner of homicide in the best Victorian tradition.

Did Mr Hangman Berry, in dispatching his phonetic

namesake in Dundee at 8 a.m. on that April morning in 1889, really, as legend has it, 'polish off' Saucy Jack? It is for each reader of Mr Macpherson's strongly argued prosecution case to reach his or her verdict. He has certainly given me reason, if not to quit, at least to shift uneasily in my seat on the bloodied fence.

Richard Whittington-Egan
2005

AUTHOR'S NOTE

IT IS NOT THE PURPOSE OF THIS BOOK TO ATTACK RIVAL THEORIES about the identity of Jack the Ripper. The purpose of this book is mainly to put a detailed examination of the Bury case down on paper for the first time. William Bury is by far the outstanding suspect for the crimes of Jack the Ripper and a detailed book about Bury has been long overdue.

Other writers who follow me can compare Bury against the other suspects. When they do, I am sure that they – like me – will find the case against William Bury by far the strongest and most compelling.

Meanwhile, readers wishing to conduct their own investigation into the Bury case should visit the West Search Room of the National Archives of Scotland in Edinburgh, where they will find the case papers (JC26/1889/15), the Justiciary transcript (JC36/3) and the Precognition of the trial (AD/89/160). A visit to the Local Studies Department of Central Library, Dundee, is also recommended.

A NOTE ON THE SOURCES

The West Search Room of the National Archives of Scotland in Edinburgh contains a transcript of the trial of William Bury and the case papers including correspondence about the case. The case itself was covered in detail by the *Dundee Advertiser* and by the *Dundee Courier*. Of the two newspapers, the *Dundee Advertiser*'s coverage of the case was the more exhaustive and can be examined on microfilm in the Central Library, Dundee. Tayside Police have a private museum within West Bell Street Police Station which also contains information about the case, including biographical data about the police officers who were involved. Other sources I have consulted include the *Dundee Yearbook 1889* and the *Dictionary of National Biography*.

For information about the Jack the Ripper murders in London, I have mainly used reports published in *The Times* in 1888. Where there has been some doubt over the names of particular individuals, I have used the names as given in *The Jack the Ripper A–Z* by Paul Begg, Martin Fido and Keith Skinner.

A NOTE ON THE QUOTATIONS

Most of the quotes are from the same sources. All quotes relating to the arrest and trial of William Bury have come either from the *Dundee Advertiser*, 12 February to 25 April 1889, the *Dundee Courier*, 12 February to 25 April, or from the transcript of the trial which is held in the National Archives of Scotland. Unless otherwise stated, all quotes relating to the crimes of Jack the Ripper have come from *The Times*, 1 September to 12 November 1888.

E.M.

PROLOGUE

THE WHITECHAPEL MURDERS OF 1888 MUST GO DOWN AS ONE of the most puzzling whodunnits in criminal history. More than 100 years on, with any number of suspects having been put under the microscope, we seem no nearer to finding the killer than we ever were. But amidst the profusion of theories for the Jack the Ripper murders, the simplest and most likely solution is the one which has been most consistently overlooked.

The problem for theorists is the sudden cessation of the murders in November 1888. What happened to make this notorious serial killer stop? It is not in the nature of serial killers to stop unless they get caught. But Jack the Ripper was never caught . . . So what could have happened to make him stop?

The simplest and most overlooked answer is that he did not stop. Instead, he moved out of the City of London and continued his gruesome career elsewhere. If we are going to look for him, therefore, we need to look for a man who was living in the East End of London in the autumn of 1888 and who also committed Ripper-style murders elsewhere.

Such a man does, in fact, exist. His name was William Henry Bury and this is his story.

Part One

DUNDEE, 1889

1

A QUIET SUNDAY EVENING

SIXTY-TWO-YEAR-OLD LIEUTENANT JAMES PARR WAS THE SENIOR officer on duty at the Central Police Office, Dundee, on Sunday, 10 February 1889. Born in Ireland in 1826, he had started out as a weaver before joining Dundee Burgh Police in 1850. The police may have been his second choice but this former failed weaver had shown a natural aptitude for a career in crime detection and had steadily risen through the ranks till, in 1881, he became 2nd Lieutenant.

At 6.50 p.m., a short, bearded man walked into the police station and asked Parr for a private interview. The man was 5 ft 3½ in. in height and was under ten stone in weight. When he took his hat off, he revealed a head of dark hair. But he would not look Parr in the eye as he spoke.

On duty with Lieutenant Parr was Constable William McKay, who was the acting bar officer. Parr left McKay in charge of the police station and took the man into a private room but did not offer him a seat. The man, who still had not given Parr his name, began to make his statement. He said that he and his wife had been drinking heavily on the night of 4 February 1889. By late evening, he was so overcome with liquor that he did not know what time he had gone to bed.

As the man continued, his statement became more and more bizarre. The next morning, he said, he had awoken at about 10 a.m. and was surprised that his wife was not in bed with him. On looking around the apartment, he saw her lying on the floor. He called to her but got no response. Getting up and going over to her, he was startled to find that she was lying dead on the floor with a rope around her neck.

The man did not attempt to summon a doctor. Instead, after looking at the body for a minute or two, he was seized with a mad impulse: lifting a large knife that lay nearby, he plunged it several times into the woman's abdomen. Some time after this, he said he became afraid that he would be arrested as Jack the Ripper. In his panic, he concealed the body in a large box.

Parr thought the man appeared quite sober, 'considering the character of his communication'. Still, the lieutenant asked the man if he had been drinking lately.

The man said he had and added that he had been staying in the house since his wife's death but had become so uneasy about the matter that he could not get peace of mind until he reported it. At this point, Parr asked the man for his name and address. The man gave his name as William Henry Bury and his address as the basement apartment at 113 Princes Street.

Parr now decided to take Mr Bury upstairs to the Detective Department, where Lieutenant David Lamb, Chief of the Detective Department at City of Dundee Police, and Detective Peter Campbell were on duty. Lamb was 50 years old and had progressed smoothly through the ranks, having joined Dundee Burgh Police Force as a constable on 2 April 1864. He had recently been awarded the sum of £1 sterling for displaying 'zeal and intelligence' in the conduct of theft cases.

Parr introduced Bury to Lamb by saying that he had a wonderful story to tell. Parr then remained present while Bury repeated his story but, this time, there were subtle differences. Bury made no mention of Jack the Ripper to Lieutenant Lamb and also said that he stabbed his wife's body only once.

Lamb asked Bury some questions 'with the view of ascertaining if he was in his sound and sober senses or under a delusion'. Bury's whole manner led Lamb to form the opinion that he was 'quite sane and collected and sober'. Lamb immediately told Parr to detain Bury downstairs while he 'went to see as to the truth of the statement'. Bury was visibly surprised when Lamb said this, as if he had expected the detective to accept his story without investigation.

Parr took Bury back downstairs to the Orderly Room, where he was searched. A small pocketknife was found in his possession. Parr then remained with Bury until 9 p.m., when he was relieved from duty. William Bury had not been charged with anything at this point and had not been arrested, either. But he was clearly not free to go. In Lamb's written statement, he said that he gave instructions for Parr to take William Bury downstairs 'in charge', whatever that might legally mean. It certainly seems to mean that a policeman was going to remain with Bury and would prevent him leaving the police station if he attempted to do so until Lieutenant Lamb returned.

When Lieutenant James Parr walked out of the Central Police Office on that quiet Sunday night, he had handed over the investigation to Lieutenant David Lamb and, as far as we can tell, took no further part in it himself. But Parr had already missed a golden opportunity to ask William Bury what he meant when he said he was afraid he would be arrested as Jack the Ripper. Moreover, if Bury had not expected to be arrested, it is logical to assume that he would not have seen the need to prepare a defence. Therefore, an opportunity to get Bury talking about Jack the Ripper when his cover story was not fully formed in his mind had just been lost.

However, neither Parr nor Lamb had any reason to connect William Bury with the Jack the Ripper murders at this stage. In fact, they did not even know for sure that a murder had been committed. Furthermore, neither Parr nor Lamb had had – for obvious reasons – any involvement in the Jack the Ripper murders. Neither of them knew the modus operandi of Jack the Ripper. Therefore, when Lamb did discover the body, he was not to know that the modus operandi of the killer was indeed very similar.

On Tuesday, 12 February 1889, the *Dundee Advertiser* concluded its report of the incident as follows:

> In the course of further conversation he [i.e. Bury] made a remark about Jack the Ripper but the Lieutenant did not understand what Bury meant and did not wish at that stage to inquire.

But the *Dundee Courier*'s version of this incident was more blunt:

> When they were alone the man, who appeared much excited, said he was 'Jack the Ripper' or 'a Jack the Ripper' or something to that effect.

Parr himself had said to journalists that Bury had said he was afraid he would be arrested as Jack the Ripper but Parr does not seem to have written down Bury's statement and so this should not be regarded as an exact quote. However, it begs the question: why was Bury afraid he would be arrested as Jack the Ripper?

It seems that Parr had not taken Bury completely seriously. Describing the interview between Parr and Bury, the *Dundee Courier* commented on 25 April 1889:

> The statement was of so horrible a nature, and the stranger's manner was so confused and excited, that the officer was at first somewhat incredulous, supposing that the man had become mentally deranged by stories of Jack the Ripper.

It could be argued that Parr's questioning of Bury was shockingly inadequate but Parr was questioning William Bury before the discovery of the body. It would later become clear that there were parallels with the Whitechapel murders but this was not obvious to Parr. To put it in a nutshell – the likelihood of Jack the Ripper turning up in Dundee and walking into a police station muttering oblique confessions would have seemed a bit of a long shot. It was simply not on Parr's mind that the infamous Whitechapel murderer might have wandered into the Central Police Office in Dundee on a cold Sunday evening in February.

Bury had finished his story by taking a key from his pocket and, handing it to David Lamb, had said, 'There's the key of the door and you will easily find the box with the body in it. The house can be easily got and you will know it at once because there are red curtains on the front window.'

Lieutenant David Lamb and Detective Peter Campbell set out for the property at 113 Princes Street, unaware of the potential ramifications of what they might find there. The men were investigating a mysterious death in Dundee and it did not occur to them that they were about to make a discovery that would have huge implications for the notorious series of murders which had recently been committed some 500 miles away.

2

THE DISCOVERY OF THE BODY

DETECTIVES LAMB AND CAMPBELL TRAVELLED BY HORSE-DRAWN carriage across the cobbled streets of Dundee city centre. They pulled to a halt outside 113 Princes Street but did not immediately go in. Instead, they knocked on the door of John Lee, Bury's next-door neighbour, and asked him to go into the house with them (presumably because he might have been required to give a statement as a witness).

The tenement blocks at Princes Street were set two or three yards back from the street. When standing on the street, you would look across a moat at the tenement. To enter from street level, you had to walk across a narrow footbridge that would take you into the main entrance from where there would be a stair leading to the upper floors. In total, the tenement had four storeys. Access to the upper three floors was via the footbridge at street level. Entrance to the basement apartment was by a different stair that dropped under the footbridge as it led from the street to the front door.

The streetlighting was poor: a few solitary gas lamps cast small pools of light at irregular intervals in the dark street and did little to lift the gloom of a dark night. The three men cautiously made their way down the seventeen stone steps that led to Bury's front door. Lamb turned the key in the lock: the door creaked open and the men stepped into a musty, cold blackness.

Lamb struck a match and got enough light from the flickering flame to see that they were in the kitchen. The kitchen, described by the *Dundee Advertiser* as 'very dingy', was bare except for a couple of bits of red curtain that hung on either side of the window.

Lamb pushed open the door of the adjoining room. A few bits of coal 'and some other articles' were still burning in the fireplace. Lamb immediately spotted a candle and lit it with his match. The candle spluttered into life, casting its yellow light around the room and revealing a large white wooden box in the middle of the floor with a pile of clothing on top of it.

Lamb noticed a spot of blood on the floor near the box. He later said that he had 'no doubt' that the floor had been washed, although he never explained why he drew this conclusion. Perhaps the floor was the only clean area in the dirty flat.

Helped by Peter Campbell, Lamb slowly removed the clothing from the top of the box. The two men then noticed that two centre boards in the lid of the box were loose. They removed both of these and a bed sheet which was covering the contents of the box. As soon as they pulled the sheet away, they could see the foot and right leg of a woman. The leg had been broken to make it fit into the box. Lamb stopped what he was doing and decided to call the police doctor immediately. He left Detective Campbell in charge of the scene and drove by carriage to the Eastern Police Station.

Thirty-one-year-old Charles Templeman had been the Police Surgeon of Dundee for the past six years. At 8.15 p.m., he received what he described as 'a telephonic message from Chief Constable Dewar' asking him to go at once to 113 Princes Street, where he would meet Lieutenant Lamb and Detective Campbell.

Templeman arrived in Princes Street at 8.40 p.m. and followed Lamb and Campbell down the steps, through the kitchen and into the bedroom. While Templeman and Campbell watched, Lamb now removed the clothing, books and other articles which had carefully been packed into the box on either side of the body. As he did so, it became apparent to the men that Bury had had some difficulty squeezing his wife's 5 ft 1 in. long corpse into the box.

The body was naked, apart from a chemise. It was lying on its back with the left leg doubled-up and twisted so that the foot rested near the right shoulder. The head had been pushed into the left-hand corner of the box and turned towards the right. Both major bones in the right leg had been broken to make it fit into the box. There was also a gaping hole in the abdomen, through which the victim's intestines were protruding, and a mark of constriction around the neck.

Only the briefest of looks was enough to tell Templeman that these injuries were not self-inflicted. He immediately gave his opinion that another medical man should be present when the body was removed from the box. The examination was immediately halted, the body was left in the box and David Lamb drove back to the Central Police Office to charge William Bury with murder. Bury's only response was a startled 'No!' before he was searched and taken down to the cells.

At the time of his arrest, Bury had in his possession 'several' gold rings, two brooches, two pairs of gold earrings, one lady's silver watch, two silver lockets and one silver chain. This was obviously the remains of Ellen Bury's jewellery, which he had not yet taken to the pawnbroker.

Lamb now called in a second medical man and returned to the scene of the crime. A cab was sent for Dr Stalker and by the time Stalker arrived, both the Chief Constable and Procurator Fiscal were also in attendance. The remaining boards or planks on the top of the box were prised open and the body was lifted out, put on a stretcher and carried to a cart that was waiting in the street. At about midnight, the body of Ellen Bury was driven to the 'deadhouse', or mortuary, for the post-mortem examination.

Meanwhile, David Lamb conducted a quick search of the apartment. He found a knife on the window sill of the room where the body was found and, in the candlelight, could see that there were small quantities of blood, flesh and hair on it. Near the box, Lamb also found a length of rope. There were several hairs on the rope and these were similar in colour to that of the dead woman. The premises were then locked up for the night and a constable was put on duty to ensure that no one entered.

But once the body was in the deadhouse, the police realised that they had a problem. No one knew who the deceased was. William Bury had said that she was his wife, Ellen, but his statement could not be corroborated. Formal identification would have to wait until members of Ellen Bury's family could be found and contacted.

On Monday morning, David Lamb and Peter Campbell returned to the house in Princes Street to examine it in daylight. They found the kitchen empty of furniture. With its bare walls and floorboards, the kitchen must have given the impression that the house had been uninhabited for some time. Only the old red curtains hanging by the window indicated that people might have lived here.

The bedroom, being sparsely furnished, was a little more welcoming. Its floor was littered with articles of clothing, books and pamphlets. A copy of the New Testament, two hymn books and a prayer book were among the objects scattered across the floor. A small edition of Johnson's dictionary was also found with an inscription on the flyleaf: 'Emma Perott, 9 Arnold Road, Bow E'.

Lamb and Campbell were specifically looking for items of clothing which had been worn by Ellen Bury. All they could find was one lady's ulster, or jacket. The ulster was bloodstained on both the inside and outside. There were also rips on either side, suggesting a considerable amount of violence had been used. Strangely, however, they could not find any other items of women's clothing and this drew them to the large pile of ashes in the fireplace. Amongst the ashes they found:

- steel portions from a woman's corset;
- four pieces of steel from the improver of a woman's dress;
- 10 metal buttons;
- the remains of a wooden tucker;
- two brooches and earrings;
- five buttons from a dress;
- the framework of a purse;
- the handle of a fancy bag;
- two sides of the bust of a corset;
- 20 hooks and seven eyes;
- four metal buttons and two bone buttons;
- 11 hairpins;
- a buttonhook;
- part of a watchchain with ornaments;
- the metal rings of three ladies' umbrellas;
- a number of keys and 'other articles'.

In Lamb's view, this indicated that 'there had recently been burnt in the fireplace considerable portions of a lady's wearing apparel and other articles belonging to a lady'.

The complete absence of furniture in the house suggested that

Bury had not merely been burning his wife's clothes in the fireplace but had, in fact, burned the chairs, mattress and whatever else might have been in the apartment.

It is possible that Bury had been trying to destroy whatever evidence there might have been in the room, although that does not explain why the police were able to find the bloodstained ulster, knife and rope. More likely is the explanation that Bury had never experienced a Scottish winter before. In a draughty house with broken windows, he may simply have been forced to chop up the furniture for firewood in an attempt to keep warm. If he had run out of money, he may not have been able to buy coal and sticks, and therefore burned whatever came to hand. Alternatively, he may have thought it too risky to allow a coalman to deliver coal to his house in case the coalman got a glimpse of the dead woman.

Back at the deadhouse, Drs Templeman and Stalker began their post-mortem examination at about 1 a.m. The examination would take three hours and seems to have been undertaken by Templeman with Stalker looking on. Templeman looked at the marks of constriction around the neck and the large wound in the abdomen through which the intestines were protruding. As he did so, he must have realised the huge burden that lay on his shoulders: there were no witnesses who saw Ellen Bury die or who could in any way dispute William Bury's story. The entire prosecution case would, therefore, have to be built around this medical examination.

The first conclusion that Templeman came to was that the case was *not* one of hanging. The marks around the neck were more consistent with strangulation. Templeman formed this opinion because the force used to strangle Ellen Bury must have been applied downwards and backwards: this suggested to him that someone had been pulling the rope from behind.

Both from the direction of the attack and the amount of force required to produce the injuries, Templeman reckoned that it would have been impossible for a right-handed woman to have caused them herself. From the position of the knot and the circular furrow that was 'well marked and all round the neck', Templeman concluded that the case was not one of hanging.

The other possible cause of death that Templeman had to discount was that of suicide by strangulation. Suicide by strangulation would have required an arrangement for the pressure to be kept up after the person lost consciousness. This could have been provided by a ligature being passed around the neck several times or being tightened by such an instrument as a stick inserted between the ligature and the neck and twisted round. Nothing of this kind had taken place in this case. It was Templeman's opinion that the force used against the victim had to have been maintained by another person after she became insensible.

Templeman also felt that several of Ellen Bury's injuries indicated that a struggle had taken place before death. There were bruises to Ellen Bury's head, including a bruise above the left eyebrow and a wound on her nose. There was an abrasion over the knuckle of her right mid-finger, which seemed to have been scooped out by a fingernail. The violence needed to cause the bruises would have been enough to stun the victim, thus rendering it easy for the killer to strangle her without her being able to fight back. Dr Templeman concluded that the wounds to the abdomen must have been inflicted either during life or at most ten minutes after death, while the victim's body retained its warmth and elasticity.

William Bury's story was that his wife had committed suicide while he was asleep and that he had woken up in the morning to find her body on the floor. This was the time when he supposedly inflicted the wounds in the abdomen – several hours after her death. His statement is clearly contradicted by Templeman's evidence.

Another contradiction is the fact that Bury said that he and his wife had been drinking heavily on the night before her death. Templeman examined the contents of the deceased's stomach and found that it contained a quantity of partially digested food 'which had a sourish but not *alcoholic* smell'.

Two knives had been found – one in the possession of the prisoner when he was searched and one in the house. Templeman's opinion was that the injuries to Mrs Bury had been inflicted by the knife that Lieutenant Lamb found in the house.

At the time of her death, Ellen Bury had been wearing a lady's jacket called an ulster. The ulster was dark brown in colour and had a hood lined with brown velvet. According to Templeman, the large quantity of blood on the ulster represented even more evidence that the wounds had been inflicted 'very near to the time of death', either before or after. The blood at the mouth of the left sleeve of the ulster suggested that the victim had put her left arm down to protect her abdomen when it was struck with the knife.

Dr Templeman had built up a clear picture of the murder. The killer had approached the victim from behind, brandishing a heavy iron implement like a poker. He had stunned her with several blows to her head. Before she was able to recover, he put the rope around her neck and began to strangle her. In attempting to fight him off, Ellen reached over her shoulder and scratched him on the wrist.

Ellen Bury lost consciousness and the killer, thinking she was dead, laid her body down on the floor. He then picked up a knife and slashed open her abdomen. As she was dying, she was still sufficiently conscious to try to protect her abdomen with her left hand.

William Bury was examined by James Miller, Dundee Prison Surgeon, on Monday, 11 February 1889. Miller spotted scratches on Bury's right wrist. Bury said that these scratches had been made by a black cat in a public house on Saturday, 2 February. Miller, however, considered this improbable. The parallel directions of the scratches and the intervals between them suggested that they had been caused by human fingernails.

Miller's hypothesis was that the victim had scratched William Bury while she was being strangled: he believed she had reached over her shoulder to try to break Bury's hold on the rope and, in so doing, scratched him on his right wrist.

The medical evidence pointed to a straightforward case of homicide. This was reinforced by the fact that two other doctors – Drs Stalker and Littlejohn – both examined the body and concurred with Templeman's findings. It may have seemed, at this point, that the case would fall under the description of 'open and shut'. The trial was fixed for Thursday, 28 March 1889.

3

'JACK RIPPER IS AT THE BACK OF THIS DOOR'

ON TUESDAY, 12 FEBRUARY 1889, THE *DUNDEE COURIER* described the excitement in the city:

> Flying rumours began to be whispered abroad that Jack the Ripper had come to Dundee and given himself up . . . in the dinner-hour when the workpeople were issuing from various public works the whole subject of the conversation was Jack the Ripper. Groups of men and women and children gathered round the newsagents' shops reading, with feelings of horror, the special bill issued by the *Courier* announcing the event. 'Ay, it's true; it's true,' was the general exclamation. 'He's given himself up,' and, 'He's a Londoner, too.' In the east end of the town crowds, actuated by a morbid curiosity, visited the scene of the tragedy. The excitement was very intense during the meal hours, and after the works closed in the evening heavy showers of snow began to fall and drove the people off the streets as the night set in.

Much of this excitement had been generated by a piece of evidence that had newly been discovered. The following is a report from the *Dundee Advertiser* of the same day:

> The scene of the fearful tragedy is a back room in a sunk tenement at 113 Princes Street, on the right-hand side

going up. The locality is inhabited chiefly by respectable working families but the rooms beneath are occupied by those of a much poorer class. The house occupied by Mr and Mrs Bury is reached by a winding stair leading by a gate through a railing which bounds the street to the sunk flat. The place has a dirty and squalid appearance and a peep through the window, in which several panes are broken and which is covered with grime, shows nothing but an empty kitchen. A pair of crimson curtains hang at the sides of the window, looking strangely out of keeping with the bareness visible everywhere else. There appears to be no grate in the fireplace, which is filled with ashes. A door leads through to an inner room in which the body was found. On going round behind it was found that the blind was closely drawn so that the interior could not be seen. The back premises are led to by a dirty stair, at the foot of which on an old door is the following written in chalk – *Jack Ripper* [*sic*] *is at the back of this door.*

At the back of this door, and just at the turn of the stair, there is the inscription – *Jack Ripper is in this seller* [*sic*].

The handwriting is apparently that of a boy and the authorities will probably attach little importance to it. But the writing is older than the discovery of the tragedy and the neighbours were startled and alarmed at the idea that one whom in their terror they associated with the Whitechapel tragedies had been living in their midst. The scene of the tragedy was visited yesterday by crowds from all parts of the city and the mural inscriptions engrossed much of the attention of the spectators.

The *Dundee Advertiser* did not explain why it attributed the writing to that of a small boy. Presumably, it did so on account of the spelling and grammatical mistakes.

It could be argued that the failure of the City of Dundee Police to attach any importance to these strange bits of graffiti was another major blunder. However, it is hard to see what use they might have made of this discovery in their prosecution of William Bury for the murder of his wife. It is, ultimately, anonymous graffiti.

There are two things we need to consider here. Was Bury the author of the writing in chalk? And if so, what relevance does it have?

Although the writing in chalk was made anonymously, it is hard to believe that anyone other than William Bury could have been the author. No one other than William Bury had entered his apartment from the time of the murder to the discovery of the body (a period of seven days). Once the murder had been discovered, there was always at least one policeman on duty at the scene of the crime, so the opportunity does not appear to have been there for a member of the public to write something on the walls of the house.

The *Dundee Advertiser* reported that the writing 'was older than the discovery of the tragedy'. The paper did not explain how it arrived at this conclusion: presumably, the chalk marks did not look like they had been newly made. The *Dundee Advertiser* also reported that the scene of the crime was visited by large crowds from all parts of the city, which explains why the rumours about Jack the Ripper being in Dundee spread so quickly through the city. But could anyone, other than William Bury, have been responsible for the writing in chalk?

Bearing in mind that no one else entered the property from the time of the murder to the discovery of the body, one is led to the conclusion that William Bury must have been the author. From 29 January, the only other person who was in the house was his wife. But she was badly educated with poor writing skills and it seems unlikely that she did it.

But what relevance does all this have? If it could be regarded as a confession then it obviously becomes highly significant. But an unsigned confession has no legal force. It is easy to see why the Dundee Police thought it had little evidential use.

However, both the local newspapers – the *Dundee Advertiser* and the *Dundee Courier* – attempted in different ways to link William Bury to the Whitechapel murders. The following report appeared in the *Dundee Advertiser* on 25 April 1889:

> Comparatively little is known of the antecedents of Bury and from the fact that he was an entire stranger in Dundee much interest has been manifested to learn anything regarding him. When he was apprehended there was a feeling in the community that he might have some connection with the atrocities which had been committed in the Whitechapel district of London and this feeling was made stronger when it became known that Bury had been

long resident in that district of the metropolis. The police immediately took up this point and wrote full particulars of the tragedy along with every detail they could learn of Bury and forwarded them to Scotland Yard with a request that full inquiries should be made regarding Bury. The London police were somewhat slow to move in the matter and from this it was inferred that they did not attach much importance to the arrest as far as the Whitechapel murders were concerned. After nearly a week had elapsed they sent down a formal communication to Chief Constable Dewar giving the result of some preliminary inquiries they had made in the district in which Bury had resided. These dealt chiefly with his general habits and character as known to his companions but no reference was made to the London murders. They, however, intimated that the investigations would be continued and subsequent communications received from them went to show that they believed Bury had no connections with the Whitechapel horrors. From the fact, however, that there have been no murders in the East End since Bury migrated to Dundee there are those in the community who still cling to the belief that he had something to do with these crimes.

On the same date, the *Dundee Courier* commented:

> The crime . . . was one of almost unparalleled atrocity, resembling in its harrowing details the recent Whitechapel tragedies. So intense was the horror and excitement in the community that the perpetrator of the crime in Princes Street was generally supposed to be the infamous 'Jack the Ripper', a surmise all the more readily to be believed when it became known that the parties had actually come from the East End of London.

On 13 February, the *Courier* proposed the slightly different theory that Bury 'had been connected with some crime in the Metropolis; that he and his wife, who was also cognisant of this, fled to Dundee, and that on account of his wife threatening to become informer he had killed her'.

Although the story ran in Dundee newspapers, it was not

picked up by any newspapers in London. It is worth bearing in mind, however, that this was not an age of instant communication. The editor of a London newspaper could be understood for taking the view that it was not worth sending a journalist up to Dundee when it would take the best part of a week for him to get there and back. Bearing in mind that no televised pictures of the writing in chalk were being beamed down to London, it may not have been clear to an editor that there was any revelatory evidence worth looking at or that the story was worth investigation.

Today, it would be normal practice for there to be an exchange of communication between the different police forces involved. In 1889 the technology did not exist for the instant transmission of photographs. Nevertheless, it seems strange that the City of Dundee Police did not telegraph Scotland Yard with a message to the effect that it might have been in their interest to interview William Bury. Today, Scotland Yard has no record in its archives of any correspondence between the City of London Police and the City of Dundee Police relating to Bury. That does not exclude the possibility that messages *were* exchanged in 1889 and have either been lost or destroyed.

But an article published in the *Dundee Courier* on 15 February 1889 may provide a clue as to Scotland Yard's apparent lack of interest in the case. The article, which quotes an interview between a *New York Herald* correspondent and 'one of the most prominent heads of the Scotland Yard Police Force', took the form of a conversation between them which went as follows:

> *New York Herald*: What do you think, inspector, about this Dundee murder?
>
> Inspector: I have no detailed information as to this case but my experience would lead me to believe that the body of the victim, Ellen Elliot, was mutilated by her alleged husband in an excess of murderous mania. That form of temporary insanity is, as you know, very common, the Whitechapel murders being a most striking illustration of the fact. Furthermore, as is unquestionably the case with Jack the Ripper, this mania is often recurrent at regular intervals.
>
> *New York Herald*: Do you credit the man's statement that he is the original Jack the Ripper?

Inspector: Not for a moment. Were he really the Whitechapel murderer stricken with remorse, we should have a detailed confession of all his crimes. As it is, he merely talks in a rambling incoherent way about being the author of the London horrors. It is not often that a criminal is so deeply moved by remorse as to make a confession but when that does happen the confession is never made by halves . . . Oh no, you can be sure the man Bury is not Jack the Ripper.

This reported interview, if accurate, seems to show an extraordinarily complacent attitude on the part of Scotland Yard. However, by the start of 1889, the worldwide press had picked up the story and seemed to be reporting any random murder anywhere across the globe as the work of Jack the Ripper. Consider the following report from the *Dundee Courier* of 23 January 1889:

Telegrams received here state that great excitement prevails at Corunna where the sudden disappearance of two girls, the elder of whom is only seventeen, has been attributed to Jack the Ripper. People affirm that the Whitechapel murderer reached the town on the 17th inst., and that he has been prowling about the place after dark ever since his arrival. Young women and girls no longer go out at night and even have their doors barricaded to keep out the mysterious assassin. It is also reported that the Whitechapel ruffian has written one of his cold-blooded epistles to authorities, telling them that he is doing his rounds and that he intends to disembowel several 'ladies' before he leaves Corunna.

The problem is that this type of newspaper story is far from unique. Less than three weeks later, on 11 February 1889, this report was printed in the *Dundee Courier*:

JACK THE RIPPER IN JAMAICA: A STRANGE STORY
The crews of the various steamers plying between New York and Kingston, Jamaica, are telling fearful stories of crimes committed in Spanish Town, a village near Kingston, which to their minds unquestionably indicate that Jack the Ripper has gone from England to Jamaica.

The first of a series of diabolical and mysterious murders took place, so the sailors say, on the 28th of November, 1888, in St Catherine's parish, a few miles distant from Spanish Town. The victim was a negress of the lowest and most vicious class, whose name has never been discovered. She was found early in the morning lying by the roadside, her throat cut from ear to ear, her cheeks, nose and forehead slashed in a manner that would indicate it to be the work of a skilful butcher. The body was mutilated exactly as had been done in the London cases. If anything further had been needed to make the horror-stricken crowd attribute the crime to the Whitechapel murderer, it was found on a card pinned to the unfortunate woman's body by the blade of a small penknife. The card bore the inscription

JACK THE RIPPER
Fourteen more, then I quit

On the morning of the 13th December, in a field, lying by and partially concealed under an old shed was found a second body. In this case the woman was a notorious creature of the lowest class, a negress called 'Mag'. Her wounds were of the same nature as those inflicted upon the other. The field in which the corpse was discovered was scarcely a mile from the scene of the first murder. The authorities made a hurried investigation and buried the body as speedily as possible, giving no one an opportunity to examine it. No mention of the crimes was made in the newspapers at the time, the officials endeavouring by every means in their power to hush the matter up and have talked about it as little as possible. No trace was ever found of the murderer and it was forgotten save by a few of the wretched women who belong to that class among which the unfortunates moved.

The third body was found on the Friday before New Year's Day. This time the newspapers were compelled to notice the discovery. The scene of this third murder was about midway between the places where the former discoveries had been made and the sailors insist that the crime was in every way analogous to the others.

For those would-be murderers who were clever enough, the closing months of 1888 provided a golden opportunity. If they could throw suspicion on Jack the Ripper, they would immediately deflect suspicion from themselves. All you had to do was kill somebody and leave a calling card by the body with 'Jack the Ripper' signed on it!

On 19 February, the *Dundee Courier* printed the following:

> It is reported from Managua, in the state of Nicaragua, Central America, that six women have been found horribly murdered and mutilated in various parts of that city. All the victims were of the class of those who met their fate at the hands of the Whitechapel murderer, and the incidents of crimes were of the same revolting character. No trace has been discovered of the perpetrator or perpetrators.

The *Courier* story went on to quote from the *Pall Mall Gazette*, which offered the following theory:

> The murders and mutilations were in all probability performed by a ship's cook, who possibly enough was a Malay, on one of the steamers plying to and from the port of London. The last Whitechapel murder was committed on Lord Mayor's Day, November 9th, since which time there have been no similar murders in the East End of London. We now learn that at the beginning of January similar atrocities were taking place in Nicaragua and that about the end of December barbarian [sic] mutilations are reported from Jamaica. It would be interesting to know whether any steamer left the Thames after the 9th of November, and after calling at Jamaica in December proceeded to Central America.

During January and February 1889, the *Dundee Courier* had carried stories that Jack the Ripper was in Spain or Nicaragua or Jamaica . . . or Dundee. That the same newspaper could carry stories of such diverse sights of the Ripper is extraordinary: if he was in Spain then surely he could not be in Jamaica? This may explain why the London newspapers did not pick up on the Dundee story: by the time William Bury had surfaced in Dundee, there may simply have been too many bogus Ripper stories circulating in the popular press.

But there may be another reason why Bury was quickly discounted as a Ripper suspect: he did not fit the preconceptions people had about the London killer. A story in the *Dundee Courier* (12 February) says as much:

> The fact that Bury and his wife hailed from London, and the similarity of the crime with the Whitechapel tragedies, gave rise in the forenoon to all sorts of rumours that the veritable 'Jack the Ripper' had at last been run to earth and that upon his own confession. This is, however, a theory which the appearance of the man and every other circumstance connected with the tragedy go to refute. That such a diminutive and fragile specimen of humanity could have been guilty of such horrible atrocities as those which occurred in London is by no means probable, and that such a wretch should be conscience-stricken and hand himself over to the police authorities much less so.

The *Courier* had therefore formed the opinion that William Bury was too small and fragile to be Jack the Ripper! The *Courier* arrived at this conclusion despite the fact that on 29 March 1889 the *Dundee Advertiser* said of Bury: 'Though not tall and not well formed, he seems to have a powerful chest and shoulders.'

4

THE PRISONER

WILLIAM HENRY BURY'S BIRTH CERTIFICATE IS VERY DIFFICULT TO read but his date and place of birth seems to have been given as 20 November 1859, in Hill Street, Stourbridge, in the West Midlands. His mother's name is given as Mary Bury, formerly Hendy (her medical records give her maiden name as Henley, not Hendy). His father's occupation and address is given as Fishmonger, at Hill Street, Stourbridge. This suggests very strongly that the Burys lived in an apartment above their fish shop. The following sketch of Bury's early life has been put together from newspaper reports published at or around the time of his arrest and from papers held by the National Archives of Scotland.

William Bury was the third child of Henry and Mary Bury, having one older brother and one older sister. When the young William was only three months old, his father died.

About six months before William was born, his 29-year-old mother seems to have had a severe nervous breakdown. When William was six months old, in May 1860, his mother was certified insane and was confined in Worcester County and City Lunatic Asylum.

Mary Bury was admitted as a pauper patient. James Sherlock, Medical Officer of the County and City of Worcester Pauper Lunatic Asylum, said of her: 'She is in a state of melancholia, depressed in mind and spirits, unable to speak or answer enquiries, is unable to control her emotions, cries frequently, has an inactive and listless appearance; is unable to perform for herself the simple duties of life.'

Of her physical health, Sherlock said, 'She is in a very feeble and exhausted condition, and appears in a very delicate state of health.'

Mary Bury's depression does not seem to have been brought on by her husband's death, although it may have been exacerbated by it. Her medical records indicate that she had been suffering from depression for 11 months at the time of her admission to the asylum. For at least eight months before William Bury's father died, therefore, his mother was suffering from depression.

On 5 May 1860, Mary Bury was examined at her father's house in Hill Street, Stourbridge, by Dr Thomas Bancks. Bancks said that 'her insanity assumes the form of melancholy, crying on every occasion when spoken to, and a disinclination to do any kind of work, wishing to remain in bed, her state is one approaching mental imbecility'.

Mary Bury remained in Worcester County and City Lunatic Asylum until her death on 30 March 1864. She was only 33 years old.

The children were probably looked after by relatives in Wolverhampton, although the facts are unclear. At William Bury's trial, Elizabeth Haynes, his former landlady in London, testified that Bury had told her he had lived with his uncle in Wolverhampton for many years. However, this is hearsay evidence and may not be completely accurate. Mrs Haynes does not seem to have been completely in command of the facts, because she gave William Bury's place of birth as Stourport, not Stourbridge.

It is not known what happened to Bury's brother and sister. When Bury was under sentence of death, his solicitor, D.J. Tweedie, petitioned the Secretary of State for Scotland in an attempt to save his life. At that time, Tweedie stated that Bury's mother had had three children (two boys and a girl) and that the other boy and girl were dead. No other facts were given.

When Bury was 16 years old, he was working in a warehouse at Horseley Fields. The name of his employer was given as 'Mr Bissell'. Whether this Mr Bissell was the owner of the warehouse or merely Bury's supervisor is not clear. Nor is it clear how long Bury worked at Horseley Fields. His next known job was with a lock manufacturer called Osbourne, who had premises in Lord Street, Wolverhampton. When employed at Osbourne's, Bury was described as being of a restless and unsettled temperament, of an irritating and quarrelsome nature and lacking in the principles which tend towards success in life. In 1884 or 1885, he lost his job at Osbourne's. He may have been sacked or he may simply have walked out.

The next sighting we have of Bury was in the summer of 1887 when he was seen selling lead pencils and key rings in the street in Snow Hill, Birmingham. It is likely that Bury, by this time, was scraping a bare living. The *Dundee Advertiser* described him as having 'a precarious existence'.

In the autumn of 1887, Bury left Birmingham and went to London.

Although there are a lot of missing pieces in the puzzle, the picture we have here suggests that Bury was someone who could not hold down a steady job. To have had reasonably secure jobs and then find himself selling pencils in the street suggests that Bury was either sacked or left his jobs of his own volition. From Horseley Fields to Snow Hill, the path he took in terms of his social standing and income was certainly downwards.

So why did Bury go to London? We can only indulge in conjecture but there is one obvious explanation. Never in his life did Bury give the impression that he wanted to work for a living. He may have simply bought into the myth that the streets of London were paved with gold and that, somehow or other, there would be easy jobs and easy money in the capital.

In fact, the poverty of London's East End was probably as bad or even worse than anything Bury had seen in Wolverhampton or Birmingham. This was a world where families of eight or ten lived together in one room. That meant everyone in a family would have to eat, sleep and wash in a space the size of a normal living room.

These people of the East End were imprisoned in their poverty while their landlords got rich. Every room in a dilapidated, crumbling tenement would be let out for sums like 5s.6d (five shillings and sixpence). A doss house in the East End was a sure fortune to its owner – 300 beds could be let out at a rent of 4d (fourpence) a day, bringing in the fantastic sum of £35 per week.

But even the beds in a doss house were let only to those who could pay. If you did not have fourpence, you were forced to tramp the streets all night. Lying down to rest, even in an alley, was difficult because a policeman on the beat would tell you to move on. It is easy to see why women whose husbands had left them or died might have turned to prostitution when the money they made on the streets would pay for a bed and some food the following day.

It is also easy to understand why the police found Jack the Ripper so difficult to catch in 1888. A labyrinth of dimly lit streets and side streets, the East End of London was exactly the kind of place where a killer could suddenly step out of the gloom and strike before disappearing into the shadows again.

The streets were narrow with high tenements on either side. Each street was crisscrossed with other streets, meaning that there were corners and crossroads everywhere. From any location in any street, a man on the run could probably go east, west, north or south – and, whichever way he went, he would be running into darkness because the street lighting was inadequate. Each street was lit by isolated gas lamps which created small islands of light amidst a sea of darkness. Each street might only have four or five gas lamps and, between each lamp, there would be long, dark patches where doorways were concealed in shadow.

Coal fires were also burning all across London. From every house and every factory, a myriad of chimneys belched out black smoke which hung in the air over the city and drifted back down into the streets. Now and again, a fog would come creeping off the Thames to mix with the smoke and create a dense smog, or 'peasouper'.

Jack the Ripper was about to give the police a reputation for stupidity which it would take them a long time to lose. In the detective fiction that followed the murders, writers like Conan Doyle often depicted policeman as brainless buffoons. It was the private detective or super-sleuth like Sherlock Holmes who could be relied on to uncover the truth.

But with hindsight some sympathy can perhaps be afforded the police. Order was kept by a large number of policemen walking the streets every night. If a policeman came across a crime being committed, he could not radio for help but could only blow his whistle to summon whatever other policemen were in the immediate vicinity. Meanwhile, a criminal could flee into the shadows without anyone getting a proper look at him.

In sexual crimes like the Whitechapel murders, there was no link between the killer and the victim beyond the fact that they met at a particular time and place. Normal investigative methods, which might be used to identify someone who had a motive to kill the victim, do not apply in a case like this. This means there were probably only three ways by which the police could catch Jack the Ripper:

- through information received;
- by catching the killer in the act;
- by catching the killer during the pursuit.

As far as we know, no one close to Jack the Ripper said anything to the police and no policeman on the beat came across the killer in the act and caught him 'red-handed'. Hence, options one and two are ruled out. The reality for the police, then, was that they depended on finding a body soon enough after a killing that, by raising the alarm and conducting a search of the locality, they might find the perpetrator in the vicinity with blood still on his clothes.

The Whitechapel murders were not exactly motiveless. They seemed to be the result of some vicious sexual impulse. However, they were committed at random. A victim was chosen only because she was plying her trade at a time when the murderer came walking down the street. A woman became a victim through her own bad luck and nothing else. She would not have previously known her killer and common motives such as revenge or robbery had to be discounted by the police. Therefore, no process of logical deduction would have led the police to the killer. No amount of interviews with friends and family of the deceased would have drawn out any useful information. Information may also have been withheld by people who saw Jack the Ripper but did not want to admit to being out on the streets at that time. If the police could not catch the Ripper red-handed, they were unlikely to catch him at all.

In the summer of 1887, William Bury was selling lead pencils in the street in Snow Hill, Birmingham. By October 1887, he was living and working in the East End of London. It was in October that he was taken on as a hawker of sawdust by James Martin of 80 Quickett Street, Arnold Road, Bromley-by-Bow. Bury contracted to pay Martin sixteen shillings a week in rent for a horse, cart and stable. He would then buy sawdust from Martin and keep what profit he made once he had sold it to public houses and butcher shops, where it would be scattered on the floor.

However, all was not quite as it seemed. James Martin lived at 80 Quickett Street with a woman called Kate Spooner. Kate Spooner's house was a notorious brothel in the area. It seems likely that Martin's sawdust business was the cover for the brothel. Martin was 38 years old in 1888 but Kate Spooner's age at that time is not known. By the time of Bury's trial in 1889, James Martin said that Kate Spooner was dead but gave no information about the cause of her death.

One of the perks of working at Quickett Street was that James Martin would let his men sleep in the stables or kitchen. So if they spent all their money on drink and could not afford lodgings, they could always doss in the warm kitchen or amongst some straw in the stables. This seems to be what Bury did during his brief spell at Quickett Street. On nights when he slept in the kitchen, he would see the women bringing men back to the brothel. One of these women was 32-year-old Ellen Elliot.

James Martin stated that William Bury was in the habit of sleeping in the stable except when he (i.e. Martin) was away from home. On those occasions, Bury slept in the house. It is not clear what Martin meant by this: Bury could either have been sleeping in the kitchen without permission or sleeping with one of the women in the brothel.

Ellen Elliot had been born at Stratford-le-Bow, East London, on 24 October 1855. She was four years older than William Bury. Very little is known about her early life beyond the fact that she was a sickly child who was often ill and rarely at school. She did not get much of an education, which meant opportunities for her were limited once she was of working age.

She spent part of her life in a workhouse and gave birth to a child. What happened to the child is unknown. Ellen's first job was with a clockmaker and she later worked in a jute mill. An aunt of hers, Mrs Margaret Birion, died in 1882 and left her a legacy of £300 – a huge sum of money in those days. Despite her lack of education, Ellen invested the money very sensibly. She purchased shares in the Union Bank of London and planned to use the dividends as a welcome supplement to her income.

In or around October 1886, Ellen became a domestic servant with James Martin. It seems likely that the term 'domestic servant' was a euphemism for 'prostitute'. It was common knowledge in the house in Quickett Street that Ellen had inherited money: the sum of £250 was talked about, which was not far from the mark. Apparently Ellen made no secret of it.

While she was working at Quickett Street, Ellen rented a room from 50-year-old Elizabeth Haynes of 3 Swaton Road, Campbell Road, Bow. If Ellen was a genuine domestic servant, we would expect her to be working long hours through the day and sleeping at night. But if she was working at night and sleeping through the day, what does that tell us about her likely occupation?

Elizabeth Haynes noticed that Ellen was never in her room at night and questioned her about it. Ellen told her that she was not sleeping in the room because she was looking after an invalid lady at night.

William Bury worked for James Martin from October 1887 to March 1888. Martin sacked Bury in March because, in Martin's words, Bury 'had appropriated some of my money'. Also in March 1888, Bury proposed marriage to Ellen Elliot and moved in with her. (Ellen Elliot told her landlady, Mrs Haynes, that she and Bury were going to get married when he moved in.)

These two events must be connected. Once Martin had sacked Bury, the option of sleeping in the kitchen or stables at Quickett Street was no longer open to him. By this time, he would have known Ellen Elliot for about six months and must have known that she had a room of her own and would have heard that she had some money.

William Bury and Ellen Elliot married on 2 April 1888 in Bromley Church. It was Easter Monday. William Bury's profession was given on the marriage certificate as 'sawdust contractor' but no profession was given for Ellen. Ellen Elliot's father was given as being 'George Elliot, licensed victualler'.

For about one month before the marriage, Bury had been living with Ellen in her room at 3 Swaton Road. This dates Bury's dismissal from Martin's employment as the first week of March 1888. However, Ellen Elliot did not leave Martin's employment until the beginning of April.

Therefore, it seems probable that Ellen continued to work as a prostitute for James Martin for one month after she became engaged to William Bury. During this time, she and Bury were living together. He was not working, meaning that the two of them must have been living off the money she made.

Presumably, he slept in her bed while she was out and would then vacate the bed for her to sleep in when she came back after daybreak.

On Saturday, 7 April, William Bury got drunk on his wife's money but was broke by 11 p.m. Presumably, he had been out drinking on his own. Even though Ellen was footing the bill, she does not seem to have gone out with him.

When William Bury returned to demand more money from his wife, he found her in bed. She refused to give him any more money.

The next part of the story is taken up by Elizabeth Haynes, who lived in the rooms directly underneath the Burys. When Mrs Haynes's daughter heard Ellen Bury screaming for help, she immediately woke her mother up. Mrs Haynes went straight to the Burys' room and pushed open the door. Although it was dark, the room was lit by a paraffin lamp burning on a chair near the bed. Ellen Bury was in bed and William Bury was kneeling on top of her, holding her down. He had a table knife in his hand and, in Haynes's opinion, 'was apparently about to cut her throat'.

As soon as Mrs Haynes opened the door, William Bury came off the bed. Mrs Haynes threatened to fetch a policeman but Bury pleaded with her not to do so and promised he would never behave violently again. Mrs Haynes walked into the room and took the knife from Bury. She then put the knife down on the dressing table.

Before Elizabeth Haynes left the room, Ellen asked her to take the key of the door and keep it. She explained that she was afraid that Bury would lock her in the room and kill her. Mrs Haynes took the key and told Ellen that she would be back if she heard any more noise. This conversation took place in front of William Bury, who said nothing. Mrs Haynes went back to her own room but heard nothing more that night. She later described Ellen Bury as being 'very frightened'.

By this time, William Bury and Ellen Elliot had been married for only five days. They should still have been madly in love with each other yet Ellen was already in fear of her life. This is no ordinary example of domestic violence.

Next morning, Elizabeth Haynes took the time to have a few quiet words with Ellen Bury. They spoke about the previous night and about William Bury. Ellen told Haynes that she had fallen out with Bury because she would not give him any money. Mrs Haynes said that she had noticed that Bury was always talking about money and always wanting Ellen to sell her shares. Whenever she refused, he would get angry and start pushing her or knocking her about.

Bury's behaviour at this time appears to be consistent with alcohol addiction. He was spending a lot, if not all, of his time drinking. Ellen's only value to him was to provide money for drink. When she refused, he would fly into a rage.

Another person who witnessed William Bury's violent treatment of his wife was James Martin. On two occasions after the wedding, Martin had met Ellen in the street and had noticed that her face was disfigured. She told him that she was being beaten by her husband. She complained that William had done nothing since he married her but frequent public houses and spend her money, and that their arguments always seemed to revolve around money.

James Martin testified that William Bury had been in the habit of getting drunk three or four times a week when he worked for Martin. But, Martin said, 'since he obtained the money from his wife, he has seldom been sober'. Martin went on to say that Bury always got drunk when he had money. While he was employed by Martin, Bury was always bragging about what he would do if he got money and how he would take Martin's business away and start up for himself. But whenever Ellen gave him money to buy sawdust for his business, he got drunk instead.

Martin also witnessed Bury assault his wife in the street. The first assault took place when William and Ellen Bury had just come out of an upholsterer's, where they had bought a rug, and were about to go into a public house. An argument broke out because Ellen refused to give William Bury money for drink. He punched her on the mouth and she would have fallen down in the street had not James Martin grabbed hold of her and pushed Bury away.

The next assault took place in a public house. Bury still owed Martin £17.13s. When James Martin saw the couple together in a public house, he went over to them and asked for his money. Ellen was about to pay him when William Bury hit her on the face and told her not to.

About one week after the marriage, James Martin turned up

at the Burys' room in Swaton Road and demanded the money he was owed. Ellen Bury paid him the money but Elizabeth Haynes must have overheard the conversation/argument because this was the moment when she discovered that Ellen Bury had been working for James Martin. Mrs Haynes knew that James Martin kept a brothel in Quickett Street.

Only now did Ellen Bury admit to Mrs Haynes that she had worked as a prostitute for James Martin for the whole of the time she had been a tenant with her. Despite Mrs Haynes learning this, she still referred to Ellen Bury as a 'quiet, respectable woman'. She evicted the Burys three weeks after the date of their marriage not because of Ellen's nocturnal activities but because William Bury frequently threatened and assaulted her. In Mrs Haynes's own words, she was 'obliged to get rid of them owing to his violence and bad language'.

Two or three days before they left Mrs Haynes's lodgings, Bury finally wore his wife down and managed to get her to agree to sell some of her shares. Chaperoned by her husband, she went into the Union Bank of London Ltd, 2 Princes Street, London, on 28 April 1888, and asked to dispose of one-sixth of her shares for cash.

The shareholding Ellen Bury had inherited had an estimated value of £300. Ellen received £39.7s.6d. The shares were sold the same day through the bank's own brokers.

Not all of the money was for William Bury to spend on drink, because Bury attempted to set himself up in business as a sawdust merchant. He bought a pony, cart and sawdust bags but the pony fell ill with the glanders and had to be sold again at a substantial loss (Ellen Bury lost nearly all the money she had paid for it). Nevertheless, Ellen bought a second pony for Bury's supposed business.

Once the Burys had been evicted by Mrs Haynes, they moved into lodgings at 11 Blackthorn Street, Bow East. There they remained for eight to ten weeks. There is no evidence of Bury being violent at this time, perhaps because he had made his wife cash in some of her shares. He continued to neglect his business and spent most of his time in public houses.

By May 1888, Bury had contracted a venereal disease which he had passed on to his wife. This seems strange, when she was the one who was involved in prostitution, but it strongly suggests that William Bury had been paying for the services of prostitutes.

As to which disease it was, we cannot say for sure, although gonorrhoea may seem more likely than syphilis. James Martin testified that Bury had told him 'he [i.e. Bury] had the venereal disease very bad in May last'. Martin also stated that Bury had admitted that he gave it to his wife, which tells us all we need to know about Bury's private life. About this time, Ellen Bury also told Kate Spooner that she had 'the bad disorder'.

Bury had taken his wife's money and repaid her by giving her a venereal disease! You might think that he would have shown some remorse or contrition but there is no sign of it. In fact, he kept pressurising her to sell the remainder of her shares. Ellen gave in to him on 7 June when she visited the Union Bank of London again. This time, with William Bury in attendance, she sold her entire shareholding. She was given a cheque for £194.7s.

Ellen's generosity made no difference to William Bury. As usual, he ignored his business and drifted from one public house to another. The problem was made worse by the fact that his business required him to take sawdust to public houses and butcher shops. Once Bury arrived at a public house, he could not sell a load of sawdust and move on; instead, he would have to stop for a drink. Hours later, he would still be there.

What is perhaps significant about this is that Bury seems to have developed the habit of not returning home every night. This may be significant because Jack the Ripper, whoever he was, had the ability to disappear after each murder.

There seem to be three possible explanations for the Ripper's almost magical ability to disappear. The first is that he lived alone and was therefore able to return home with bloodstained clothing without being seen. The second is that someone in his family covered up for him. And the third explanation is that the Ripper was able to take refuge in one of the many common lodging houses in the East End after each murder. The third explanation is probably the most likely, because it explains how he was able to vanish into thin air with the police often in hot pursuit.

If William Bury was not returning home every night, it clearly shows that he had another place to go. Probably, he had *more* than one place to go. He could have slept in a lodging house or he could even have slept in his cart.

Evidence that William Bury was absent from home overnight comes from James Martin. Martin recalled being in a public house at Campbell Road, Bow, on 28 December 1888. It was between half past five and six o'clock in the morning when he noticed Ellen Bury looking in through the door. She spotted Martin and came over to speak to him, telling him that William Bury had not returned home for two consecutive nights. She was worried and was wondering where her husband was.

While they were talking, Martin looked out of a window and spotted William Bury in the street. He was coming towards the public house. Martin said, 'There is Bill.' Ellen went to the door to meet him. As soon as William Bury saw her, he struck her two or three times on the face until she fell down.

This incident does not prove that William Bury was Jack the Ripper but it does prove that, like the Ripper, Bury had the ability to go missing for two or three days at a time. It also tells us that he was out wandering the streets about 5.30 a.m. Whoever killed Annie Chapman (the second victim of Jack the Ripper) was wandering the streets at this time.

Margaret Corney, Ellen's sister, stated that in August 1888 the Burys left Blackthorn Street and went to Wolverhampton. It was reported in the *Dundee Advertiser* on 12 February that the Burys had gone to Wolverhampton for one week but Corney actually stated at the trial that they went to Wolverhampton for a fortnight. This 'holiday' seems to have been born of a desire by William Bury to show his relatives in Wolverhampton how successful he was now that he was in London. He told them that his wife was the daughter of a London publican of considerable means. This was only partially untrue: Ellen was the daughter of a publican although her 'considerable means' amounted only to the savings she had accrued and that William Bury was busy spending.

While he was in Wolverhampton, Bury threw money around theatrically. For example, he took the opportunity to show off by asking a friend to cash a £50 note for him. He described himself as a 'sawdust and silver sand merchant' of Sunbury Street, London, and handed out business cards and photographs of his wife and himself.

It may be that revenge was the motive behind William Bury's generosity. During his years in Wolverhampton, he had probably been told repeatedly that he would never make a success of his life. Coming back later and flashing £50 notes was his way of getting back at his relatives: now he was the one who appeared to be the big success.

It is important, at this point, to establish the timing of events. If William Bury was in Wolverhampton when Jack the Ripper was active in London, then it becomes obvious that Bury *cannot* have been the Ripper.

William Bury and Ellen Elliot married on 2 April 1888. Three weeks later, they were evicted by Elizabeth Haynes. They then took lodgings at 11 Blackthorn Street for 'eight to ten weeks'. Assuming that there was no significant gap between the two tenancies, this puts them in Blackthorn Street approximately for the months of May and June 1888. If they immediately went to Wolverhampton on leaving Blackthorn Street, then it means they must have been in Wolverhampton for the first week of July 1888 and not August as stated by Margaret Corney.

Corney also stated that Ellen had bought 'railway shares' with the inheritance she received from her aunt. But Ellen had actually bought shares in a bank. If Corney could get mixed up over railway or banking shares, it may suggest she did not have a very good memory and was not totally in command of the details of the case. It is possible she also made a mistake with the date of the Burys' trip to Wolverhampton.

William Smith, Bury's landlord at 3 Spanby Road, Bromley-by-Bow, testified that the Burys rented three rooms from him on 11 August 1888. This puts them back in London by that date but means the holiday in Wolverhampton could have taken place any time from the first week in July to the first week of August 1888.

Margaret Corney only gave three addresses for the Burys between April 1888 and January 1889: Swaton Road, Blackthorn Street and Spanby Road. But it is obvious that there is a whole month missing. They were married on 2 April and evicted by Mrs Haynes three weeks later. This puts the date of the eviction at or around the 23 April. They then spent eight or ten weeks in Blackthorn Street. This takes us to 2 July 1888 at the latest. But they may have left Blackthorn Street as early as 18 June. They then spent a week in Wolverhampton. If they left Blackthorn Street to go to Wolverhampton, as seems logical, it means they were in Wolverhampton approximately from 2 to 9 July 1888. However, the next we know about their whereabouts is that they were back in the East End of London, where they rented rooms from William Smith on 11 August.

All of this is complicated by the fact that it is not clear when the Jack the Ripper murders actually began. The first murder is generally thought to have been that of Mary Ann or 'Polly' Nichols on 30 August 1888. Bury lived at Spanby Road, Bow, from 11 August 1888 to 21 January 1889. That means Bury was living in the East End of London when the five Ripper murders were committed.

An earlier murder was committed on 6 August 1888. It is not clear whether or not it was one of the Ripper murders. Nor is it clear where William Bury was on 6 August 1888. Either the dates as reported are inaccurate, or the Burys held a one-month tenancy somewhere that has not been reported. All we know for certain is that they did not take lodgings with William Smith till 11 August 1888.

Evidence that Corney might have got it wrong about the dates comes from the trial of William Bury in Dundee. Bury's defence counsel, the advocate Mr William Hay, cross-examined Margaret Corney and strongly suggested that she did not have all the facts at her command. The dialogue between Hay and Corney ran as follows:

> HAY: What was she [i.e. Ellen] doing for a living during the year before she was married?
> CORNEY: She was a needlewoman, made ladies' waterproof cloaks, and from there she went to a jute factory in London.
> HAY: When did she go to live with the woman Elizabeth Haynes?
> CORNEY: About two years. She had a single room in that house.
> HAY: Do you know a man called James Martin?
> CORNEY: Yes; I have seen him.
> HAY: Did he live with a woman called Kate Spooner?
> CORNEY: I knew her by the name of Kate just.
> HAY: Is that house a brothel?
> ADVOCATE-DEPUTE: Well, My Lord –
> LORD YOUNG: I won't object.
> HAY: Was it a brothel?
> CORNEY: I have heard so. I have been in Martin's house.
> HAY: Was it not in that house that the prisoner met your sister first?
> CORNEY: Yes, sir; I believe so.
> HAY: Did you know him before he married your sister?

CORNEY: I had seen him twice before he married my sister.

HAY: In her company?

CORNEY: Yes.

LORD YOUNG: In that house?

CORNEY: Yes, sir.

LORD YOUNG: And these are the only times you saw her in his company before their marriage?

CORNEY: Yes, that is all.

HAY: After their marriage, did they not take a small house near Martin's in Quickett Street?

CORNEY: I never heard of it.

LORD YOUNG: What is the name of the street that Martin lives in?

CORNEY: I never heard the name of the street.

HAY: Are you not aware that they took the lower flat of a house in Quickett Street?

CORNEY: I never heard of that.

Margaret Corney stated on oath that she had never heard the name of the street that James Martin lived in yet she also said that she had been in his house. This is not credible evidence. She probably also knew that her statement that Ellen was a needlewoman, made ladies' waterproof cloaks and worked in a jute mill during the year prior to her wedding was also untrue. Ellen had told her landlady that she was looking after an invalid so it seems logical that she would have given the same story to her sister – unless, as is more likely, her sister already knew that Ellen was a prostitute. For Margaret Corney to say that Martin's house was a brothel and that her sister met the prisoner there yet also deny that her sister was a prostitute is simply not credible. However, it was the Victorian era and Margaret Corney may not have wanted it to become public knowledge that her sister was a prostitute.

It is also odd that Margaret Corney knew nothing about the Burys living in Quickett Street. If this had something to do with Ellen's activities as a prostitute, then that alone may explain Margaret's apparent amnesia. The only problem here is that the obvious source for the Quickett Street story is Mr Hay's client – William Bury, a proven liar. Moreover, it was obviously in William Bury's interests to make Margaret Corney look like an unreliable witness.

Tellingly, perhaps, Margaret Corney did not actually deny that the Burys had stayed in Quickett Street. Her response was to say, 'I never heard of that'. If she had been confident that she knew all of Ellen's addresses during the summer of 1888, she would have denied that her sister stayed in Quickett Street. For her to say she never heard of that suggests either that she did not know or that she did know and did not wish to say.

We have already seen that there is a month missing from Margaret Corney's version of events and it may be that William and Ellen Bury lived in Quickett Street for one month while Ellen plied her trade as a prostitute. Unfortunately, we do not know when this might have been: it could have occurred any time from their eviction by Mrs Haynes to the start of their tenancy with William Smith.

Margaret Corney also made no mention of Sunbury Street as an address of the Burys during this period – yet this is what William Bury printed on the business cards that he passed around the members of his family in Wolverhampton. Again, we should remember that William Bury was not the kind of man who could be relied on to always tell the truth. If he wanted to impress his relatives, he might have invented Sunbury Street as a business address. Nevertheless, it is possible that the Burys stayed both in Quickett Street and in Sunbury Street in the summer of 1888 – either known or unknown to Margaret Corney.

Margaret Corney said at the trial that the Burys went to Wolverhampton for a fortnight in August. This is impossible because we know that the Burys were back in the East End of London from 11 August. They could have gone to Wolverhampton for one week at the beginning of August. But if they went for a fortnight, they must have gone in July.

It may well be that Margaret Corney was not in frequent contact with her sister before October 1888, when it was becoming obvious that Ellen was experiencing marital difficulties. This is supported by the fact that Margaret does not seem to have been invited to her sister's wedding. It was the landlady, Mrs Haynes, who was asked to be a witness. The name of the other witness is very hard to read but appears to be something like 'T. Tollpie'. Most certainly, the name of the other witness is not 'M. Corney'.

Probably, there was not much contact between the sisters from

April to October 1888. It may have been William Bury's violence that made Ellen go to her sister for help and emotional support – because she had nowhere else to go, even among the members of her own family. Even though William Bury was violent towards Ellen from the first week of their marriage, it took Ellen six months to go to her sister. This also suggests that the sisters were not close.

Margaret Corney's evidence can probably be considered reliable for events that occurred during or after October 1888. For these events she gives a first-hand account. But for events that occurred before October, she seems to be weak on the detail and may be giving second-hand accounts or hearsay evidence. To recap, she thought Ellen owned railway shares when in fact they were banking shares; she thought Ellen and William Bury went to Wolverhampton for a fortnight in August when it has been proved that this was impossible.

What all of this means is that we cannot identify the exact week or fortnight when William Bury was in Wolverhampton. All we can say is that he went there some time between the first week of July and the first week of August.

The reason for examining all this detail is very simple: the crimes of Jack the Ripper were to begin in August 1888. Whoever he was, he had to be in or near to the East End of London from August 1888 onwards.

5

'DON'T ILL-USE THE POOR GIRL'

ON 11 AUGUST 1888, WILLIAM AND ELLEN BURY RENTED THREE rooms from William Smith, paying 5s.3d a week. Although William Bury described himself as a sawdust and silver sand merchant, Smith stated that during the whole of the time he resided at Spanby Road, Bury was constantly drinking and very frequently drunk 'with the exception of Sundays'. Smith's evidence reads remarkably like that of James Martin and Elizabeth Haynes. Smith testified that William Bury frequently assaulted his wife and that he (i.e. Smith) often saw her face disfigured from his violence. On one occasion, Smith heard Ellen Bury screaming and had to intervene to prevent William Bury assaulting her. Echoing a phrase used by Elizabeth Haynes, Smith described Ellen Bury as a 'quiet, respectable woman' whom he only saw the worse for drink on one occasion.

Ellen Bury does not seem to have had much contact with her sisters during this time. There were four sisters: Margaret, Ellen, Charlotte and Emily. There was also a brother called George. When their aunt, Mrs Margaret Birion, died in or around 1882, she left legacies of about £300 each to Ellen, Charlotte and Emily. Margaret and George must have incurred their aunt's displeasure in some way because no money was left to them. Ellen decided to invest the money by buying shares in the Union Bank of London. At the time of the murder, Margaret Corney was 36 years old and Ellen was 32. The ages of Charlotte, Emily and George are not known.

Although Ellen Bury was living in a constant state of fear from early April, she does not seem to have spoken about her marriage to anyone until October 1888. What happened was that William Bury visited Margaret Corney one Wednesday about six o'clock in the morning to tell her that his wife was ill. Margaret went to see her sister and found her lying in bed.

Ellen told Margaret that William Bury had come home the previous Monday night and had hit her on the nose and mouth. Her mouth had swelled up and Margaret guessed that either Ellen's mouth or nose had been bleeding after the attack because there was blood on the walls of the passage, which was where Ellen said the attack took place. Clearly, this had been no mere slap: William Bury had hit his wife with enough force to break the skin and spray blood on to the wall.

Margaret was taken aback because she had not previously known that there was anything wrong with her sister's marriage. Bury had previously concealed his temper from Margaret. On the few occasions when they met, he had put on an act of being pleasant to her and apparently being pleased to see her. At the trial, Margaret Corney admitted to being fooled by William Bury and said of William and Ellen: 'They seemed comfortable and happy. When we were alone, she told me they were very unhappy.' She then added, 'He [i.e. William Bury] was very unkind to her.'

But Margaret was now very concerned about her sister. As soon as she left Ellen, she went looking for William Bury with the intention of having a few words with him. She found him later that day in his backyard and spoke about his treatment of Ellen. She was careful to protect Ellen by telling Bury that his neighbours had told her he was in the habit of hitting his wife. Bury completely denied this and Margaret was forced to leave him with the warning, 'Don't ill-use her; don't ill-use the poor girl.'

By this time, William Bury was sleeping with a penknife under his pillow. His motive may have simply been to frighten Ellen, who repeatedly found it when she was making the bed. Every time Ellen asked Bury about the knife, he denied putting it there.

Bury's behaviour at this time shows a complete lack of conscience: he gave his wife a venereal disease, stole from her and was repeatedly violent to her. But at no time did he show any remorse. This is consistent with him having a psychopathic personality.

Nor does it seem to have bothered him that he was violent in public where there were witnesses. But this did not stop him making absurd denials. He denied putting a penknife under his pillow when it was obvious that no one else could have done it. He denied hitting Ellen to Margaret Corney even though he knew several witnesses had seen him hit his wife (e.g. James Martin, Elizabeth Haynes, William Smith).

In summary, William Bury was violent. He was also a thief, a liar and a drunk. He was a completely selfish individual who was incapable of acting in the best interests of others. When he did apparently act in the best interests of others, it was because he had an ulterior motive.

Ellen visited her sister Margaret about a fortnight before Christmas. She brought all her jewellery with her, carrying it in a market basket. She told Margaret that she had to take all her jewellery with her because it was not safe to leave it behind. William Bury had threatened to pawn all her jewels – presumably for drinking money – and she had no doubt that he would do so if given the chance.

Ellen was very proud of her jewels. She had a collection of rings and brooches. It is not known what stones were in the jewels but this collection was the only thing in Ellen's life that gave her any pleasure. She liked to spend an evening spreading her jewels out on the table and polishing them.

On this occasion, Ellen went on to tell Margaret that Bury had demanded money from her the previous night because he wanted to go for a night out. When she refused, he sneaked behind her and lifted her purse out of her pocket. Then he emptied the purse and gave it back to her. Ellen told Margaret that this was not the only occasion on which he had done something like this.

Margaret, who still only knew half the story, told Ellen to leave William Bury and go before a magistrate for protection. Ellen said that she was only waiting for him to mark her again and then she would do exactly that. Margaret was not happy about this because she knew there was a real danger of Ellen being badly hurt and she urged her sister to leave Bury immediately. Ellen refused. It was a decision that was to cost her her life.

William Bury did not hit his wife again. For the next six weeks, he was to become the caring and dutiful husband.

The last known Ripper murder occurred on 9 November 1888.

It may be coincidence but the change in William Bury's behaviour manifested itself sometime after that date. With hindsight, the reason for this change seems clear: he had decided to murder his wife but knew he could not do it in London because several people would go to the police and make statements about his domestic violence. He wanted to get her out of London but also knew that she might not go with him if he continued to beat her.

From early December, William Bury had been talking about going abroad. He told William Smith, his landlord, that he was going to Brisbane and asked Smith to make him two large packing cases. In particular, Bury told Smith to make a 'good strong box that would fit quite close'. Bury wanted the box to be well secured with iron bands at the ends and about 3 ft by 3 ft by 2½ ft. This box was to be the larger of the two and Smith thought it strange that Bury should want a box like that. He asked Bury several times what such a large box was needed for. Bury replied that he was going to Brisbane and thought it would be useful to put things in. He asked Smith to stencil the words 'Bury, Brisbane' on the box but later cancelled the order. Smith duly nailed the boxes together, never suspecting that Bury planned to use the larger box as a coffin for his wife.

Margaret Corney saw her sister alive on only three more occasions. The first was on New Year's Day, 1889, when Margaret and her husband were visited by William and Ellen Bury. The women, however, had no opportunity to speak privately as William Bury remained with them for the duration of the visit. The next occasion they saw each other was on Friday, 18 January, but again the women had no opportunity to speak privately.

The story that Bury had given William Smith about Brisbane seems to have been a red herring. It was to the busy Scottish port of Dundee that Bury intended to go on Saturday, 19 January. Margaret Corney was told about this only on the afternoon of the previous day. This, too, was probably part of Bury's plan since it left Margaret Corney with little or no time to talk to her sister or attempt to dissuade her from going to Dundee.

On the afternoon of 18 January, Bury bluntly announced to Margaret Corney that he had been offered employment in Dundee. The offer consisted of a seven-year contract with a jute firm called Malcolm, Ogilvy & Co. Ltd. Margaret Corney asked

Bury how he got the job and he gave the vague answer, 'By enquiries'. He went on to say that he was to begin work on Monday, 21 January.

Bury did not show Margaret Corney the letter he claimed to have received from Malcolm, Ogilvy & Co. Ltd. And a letter, though forged by Bury, did in fact exist. Ellen's ill health meant that she had missed out on an education and did not have the ability to spot the forgery. But Margaret Corney might have noticed that there was something odd about the letter: it was clearly in Bury's own handwriting.

The forged letter, which was adduced as evidence at Bury's trial, contained errors and read as follows:

> January 12, 1889
>
> We, Messrs Malcolm, Ogilvy & Co. Ltd., Dundee, do hereby agree to take into our employ W.H. and E. Bury of No. 3 Spanby Road, London E., for a period of 7 years. Wages for W.H.B. £2 per week; wages for E.B. £1 per week. To enter on duty as soon as possible. Travelling expenses will be allowed after one month from date of entering employ.
>
> Messrs Malcolm, Ogilvy & Co.
>
> Dundee
>
> W.H. Bury
>
> Pro Tem Ellen Bury
>
> Witness – William James Hawkins.

The first mistake William Bury had made was to misspell the name of the company. The correct spelling was 'Malcolm, Ogilvie & Co.' Bury's second mistake was his failure to realise that Malcolm, Ogilvie & Co. was not a limited company. Needless to say, the company did not have an employee by the name of William James Hawkins. It is unlikely that Ellen Bury would have noticed any of these errors and she probably had insufficient education to notice the oddness of such a short letter in poor grammar which gave such scant details yet purported to be a contract. For example, the type of work which the Burys were supposedly being contracted to do is not mentioned and their job titles are not given. It is also odd that nowhere on the letter is the business of the contractor mentioned. The real Malcolm, Ogilvie & Co. of Dundee proudly described themselves as 'Jute Spinners and Merchants'.

But the most obvious indicator that the letter was a forgery was the paper it was written on – blue-lined paper with a margin on the left and columns on the right for adding up figures. It strongly resembled a blank page cut out of a diary or ledger. Most certainly, it was not the kind of paper that would be used for business correspondence. At the trial, David Rattray Malcolm of Malcolm, Ogilvie & Co. bluntly stated that the letter was not a convincing forgery.

But despite the sloppiness of the forgery, Bury's story probably did not seem unreasonable at the time. The jute industry was thriving in Dundee in 1888. There were also jute mills in Whitechapel and it was known for jute workers to drift from Whitechapel to Dundee and vice-versa looking for work. It may have been from the conversation of mill workers in public houses that Bury learned about the existence of Malcolm, Ogilvie & Co., Dundee.

Before Ellen Bury left the Corneys' house, she gave her sister a small looking-glass that had belonged to their mother. This parting gift could only have had sentimental value for the women but it is no less poignant for that. Then William and Ellen Bury left Margaret Corney and went back to Spanby Road to pack their belongings. Once they had finished, William Smith noticed that the larger case was nearly empty and contained only a few sheets and some papers. This aroused Smith's curiosity and drove him to ask Bury yet again why he needed such a large box. Bury replied, 'I shall have more things to put into it when I get to the docks.' Smith asked, 'What dock are you going to?' Bury responded, 'Ah, that's what you want to know – like a lot more.'

That evening, Bury took his wife to Clement's Coffee House in Bow and they slept there overnight. Next day, they went down to the Dundee Wharf at London Docks where they boarded the steamer SS *Cambria*. While Bury was down on the dock, supervising the loading of his boxes, Margaret Corney managed to speak to her sister for a few moments.

The women were in the cabin together and Margaret asked Ellen if she really wanted to go to Dundee. Margaret added that she should let William go on his own at first to see how he got on: he could always send for her at a later date if he was doing well. According to Margaret Corney, Ellen looked very miserable and obviously wanted to stay near her family and friends in

London. She told Margaret that Bury had said he could not go without her.

Margaret did her best to persuade Ellen not to go. She said that she would not have gone, had she been in Ellen's position. She also asked Ellen if she was sure that Bury had got a situation in Dundee. Ellen replied by saying that she did not think William had lied.

Margaret's next remark was eerily prophetic. She said to her sister, 'I'll never likely see you any more.' The last Margaret saw of her sister was when the women waved goodbye to each other as the ship pulled away from the quay. Margaret's last memory of her sister was of Ellen standing on deck wearing a brown dress trimmed with velvet, a long black velvet jacket, a black laced hat and a scarlet cravat.

Not one of Charlotte, Emily or George had come to bid farewell to their sister. The SS *Cambria* set sail down the Thames, heading for the open sea. Margaret Corney walked home alone.

6

43 UNION STREET, DUNDEE

THE CITY THAT THE BURYS WERE TRAVELLING TO MUST HAVE seemed like a small town in comparison with London. According to the 1881 census, Dundee had a population of 142,154. However, it was a busy industrial port doing business with both India and the USA. During the previous half-century, Dundee's prosperity had been built around the jute industry: jute was imported from India, spun into canvas and then exported to North America, where it covered the wagons that were rolling across the Wild West. In 1889, 1,205,730 bales of jute would land in Dundee docks.

The jute mills were the major employer of female labour in the city. In 1901, 73.5 per cent of all occupied females were working in the textile industry. So the Dundee the Burys came to in 1889 was a successful and prosperous place – at least in the comparison with the East End of London. There was work in the city for those who were fit and healthy but unskilled. But the available work in the docks or in the mills was hard, physical work: whether or not there was work for a frail woman and a hard-drinking man was another matter.

The Burys had travelled to Dundee as second-class passengers. They kept very much to themselves and did not attract much attention. Jane Guild, a 25-year-old stewardess on board the *Cambria*, spoke briefly to Ellen Bury, who told her that they were moving north because her husband had got a situation in Dundee. She did not speak to William Bury. The ship arrived in Dundee on Sunday, 20 January, and the Burys remained on board overnight, departing early on Monday morning. The next time Jane Guild saw Ellen Bury was when she was asked by police to identify the body, before the formal identification by her family.

Shortly before nine o'clock in the morning, the Burys called on Mrs Jane Robertson of 43 Union Street who had rooms to let. Union Street was close to the harbour and could have been reached by the Burys about ten minutes after coming ashore. Presumably, they were stopping people in the street and asking about lodgings. Someone had directed them to Mrs Robertson's.

Mrs Robertson's accommodation was nicely furnished and slightly more expensive than most. She took them up to the third floor of her Union Street tenement and showed them a room. The Burys agreed to move in at the rent of eight shillings a week which was for use of the room, fire, light and attendance. ('Attendance' meant that Mrs Robertson would come into the room every day to clean out the grate and do whatever other duties might have been required.)

While the Burys stayed with Mrs Robertson, their luggage comprised two large boxes. But one of these boxes was always kept padlocked and was never opened. It aroused Mrs Robertson's daughter's curiosity or suspicion so much that she commented on it to the police when the body was discovered.

On Monday afternoon, the Burys sat down at the table in Mrs Robertson's room and wrote a letter to Margaret Corney in which they described their journey to Dundee. The letter was in William Bury's handwriting but that was neither unusual nor sinister since Margaret would have known of her sister's difficulties with reading and writing:

> 43 Union Street
> Dundee
> Monday afternoon
>
> My Dear Sister
> According to my promise, I will just send you a few lines to let you know that we have arrived and also to give you our present address. Our journey was without anything occurring to mar our pleasure until Saturday night about 8.30 when the ship began her game of pitching, tossing and rolling which she did not leave off doing until about seven o'clock on Sunday night. I remained in bed all day

on Sunday up till about eight o'clock. In fact, I had all my meals in bed. I was very queer but not a bit sick and had all my meals as usual. But poor Will he got precious sick from about nine o'clock Saturday night till he landed. Eating nothing, of course. We got in about 8.30 Sunday night but, having no place to go, we arranged to remain in the ship all night and got a room this morning. I think I shall like the place as it is a very clean town and seems a busy one too. Kind regards to all my relations, not forgetting yourself and Charley.

I beg to remain your affectionate sister,
ELLEN BURY
P.S. You must please excuse this being so short. The post leaves here too early for London. Write before Friday.

But Ellen did not keep her word. Margaret Corney never heard from her sister again.

According to the forged offer of employment from Malcolm, Ogilvie & Co., William Bury was supposed to start work that Monday morning. Yet another disappointment was in store for Ellen when she learned that he did not have a job, after all.

We do not know what passed between them but, bearing in mind that William Bury rarely spoke a truthful word in his life, we can safely assume that he did not admit that he had lied to her or that the letter was a forgery. The mistake would have been someone else's but not his.

What happened next is a little surprising. Once Ellen realised that William Bury did not have a job in Dundee, why did she remain with him? She made no effort to return to London. He made no effort to look for work. Meanwhile, they continued to live on her savings. But one explanation may be Bury's change of behaviour. He no longer threatened or assaulted his wife. Ellen may have decided that the trip north to Dundee had been good for him.

The Burys stayed in Jane Robertson's property for eight days. During that time, they seemed to live happily together and frequently went out. There were two public houses in Union Street and William Bury visited both. The first public house was on the ground floor of the tenement the Burys occupied and was managed by John Burden MacIntyre, who remembered Bury and his wife visiting occasionally and having a glass of beer at the counter. The second public house was a short distance away, at 47 Union Street, and was owned by David Mackie. William Bury seemed to prefer drinking in Mackie's bar and went there for a glass of beer at least once a day. Ellen Bury came with him on only one occasion; it is not known what she drank. Amidst general bar room talk, Bury once explained that he had come north for his wife's health. But his story had changed: whereas before he said he was coming north for work, now it was for his wife's health.

On Wednesday, 23 January, William and Ellen Bury attended an evening service at St Paul's Episcopal Church, Dundee. Afterwards, they spoke to the Reverend Edward Gough. (Coincidentally, the Reverend Gough had previously preached in Wolverhampton but Bury had never attended his church there and Gough therefore did not know anything about him.)

With Ellen Bury standing by his side, William Bury told Gough that he and his wife had been living in Bow, where they had been members of the Church of England. Gough immediately asked for an introduction from a London clergyman. Bury did not have one and tried to explain this away by saying that there had been several churches within reach of their room in Bow and that they had attended each one in turn. This, Bury claimed, was the reason they were not known to any particular clergyman. But Bury's story must be regarded as bogus. Not one witness in London came forward to say they had ever seen him in a church.

Bury now brought the conversation around to the crux of the matter and asked Gough to get him a job in Dundee. He said he was in the sawdust business and had come to Dundee to look for employment.

It is possible that the Reverend Gough could have helped Bury find a job. All sorts of people would have attended his church, including wealthy businessmen. In 1889, a minister of religion did have a lot of influence within his parish. But Gough did not want to give a reference for a man he knew nothing about and whose story he may have regarded as suspicious. He did not offer to make enquiries on Bury's behalf nor did he give Bury any definite help. However, he did suggest that Bury might try the shipyards and the docks.

Gough must have asked about their situation because Bury

told him they were not in immediate want as they had 'a good large sum of money laid by'. Bury told Gough they were in lodgings in Union Street but expressed his intention to move as the rooms were too expensive.

About one week later, Gough bumped into the Burys at the top of Union Street. (Union Street was a busy thoroughfare which led from the High Street to the docks.) William Bury appeared dejected and talked about his failure to get a job. Gough told him not to give up but to keep trying, although, again, Gough does not seem to have offered any practical help.

Bury told Gough they were going to take a house to themselves. This was the last occasion Gough saw either of them before the murder. At the trial, Gough described Ellen Bury as 'a quiet-looking person' and added that 'she spoke very little'.

But was Bury really dejected about his failure to get a job? Nothing about his past history suggests that he liked working or had the ability to hold down a steady job. When he was in London, much of the time he could have spent working was spent in public houses.

It seems more likely that Bury had no intention of getting a job but wanted to be seen looking for one. The image he consistently presented to people in Dundee (neighbours, shopkeepers, publicans, the Reverend Gough) was of a thoughtful husband who cared about his wife. Mrs Jane Robertson was so taken in by Bury that she gave a statement to the police that she thought the Burys were happily married. The Reverend Gough had seen a William Bury who was supposedly dejected because he could not find work and support his wife, whom he was always seen with.

If William Bury had murdered his wife in London, he would have been the only suspect. It looks like he was trying to create a situation in Dundee where he would *not* be a suspect: nobody had seen him behave violently towards his wife nor had anyone even heard him shout at her.

Although the Burys had told the Reverend Gough they intended to leave their lodgings as the rooms were too dear, they carried on living in Union Street very much in the style of a couple who were well-to-do. They were seen wearing different clothes at different times of the day and sometimes wore three different pairs of boots and shoes in the same day. Ellen Bury often wore a sequined velvet jacket, red cravat and a dark hat.

William Bury was in the habit of wearing a tweed suit and felt hat in the forenoon while in the afternoon, after dinner, he often changed into a satin hat and black coat.

To Mrs Jane Robertson, the Burys seemed to be the stylish man- and woman-about-town. They gave her the impression that they had plenty of money to spend and were often out of their room – always going out together, with only two exceptions. This statement was contradicted in part by Margaret Robertson – Mrs Robertson's 26-year-old daughter – who said 'they occasionally walked out together and sometimes separately'.

On several evenings, either one or both of them was slightly the worse for drink but they were always quiet. Margaret Robertson stated that, as far as she saw, William Bury and his wife lived very happily together. This time her statement was supported by Mrs Jane Robertson, who said Mr and Mrs Bury 'seemed to be on very affectionate terms'.

Besides frequenting the public houses in Union Street, William Bury was also in the habit of bringing back bottles of beer to their lodgings. On one of these occasions, Margaret Robertson offered Bury the use of a corkscrew. Bury declined, saying he already had one. But although Bury was still drinking, his behaviour was much more self-controlled. Rather than being in the public house all day, he was going out for a single glass of beer and then returning. And even though he was drinking, he was quiet in the evenings.

Although William Bury had got his hands on Ellen's money, he does not seem to have pawned her jewellery. However, we have no record of her belongings at the time of her marriage: we know only that he had threatened to pawn her jewels when they were in London and Ellen took this sufficiently seriously to carry her valuables about in a basket.

On one occasion when Mrs Jane Robertson entered the Burys' room to attend to the coal fire, she noticed that Ellen Bury had proudly spread a number of gold and silver watches and chains out on the table. Ellen always carried a gold watch and chain with her and was also seen wearing what was described as a handsome brooch with earrings to match.

At about 10 a.m. on the morning of Monday, 28 January, Mrs Robertson went into the Burys' room to ask for her eight shillings' rent. Something happened that frightened her so much that she left the room without collecting her rent and never went back in while the Burys remained there.

It began with William Bury trying to beat down the rent by two shillings a week. It seemed to Mrs Robertson that the Burys had plenty of money: she was surprised to find them haggling over the rent and refused to be beaten down, thinking that they could afford the eight shillings a week.

Mrs Robertson then walked out of the room and asked her daughter to attend to her lodgers. Mrs Robertson explained that she was afraid of the man, owing to him 'looking wickedly at her'.

You would expect a landlady like Mrs Robertson to be used to dealing with different types of tenant. It seems strange that she would be afraid of a man because he looked 'wickedly' at her. But something about William Bury's manner had unnerved her. Margaret Robertson went into the room and Bury told her that the rent was more than he could pay and that he had seen furnished accommodation elsewhere for six shillings a week. No more is recorded of the conversation Margaret Robertson had with William Bury but it seems they reached an agreement that the Burys would leave the Robertson lodgings the following morning.

William Bury's story that he could not afford the rent of eight shillings may well have been true. His wife's savings would not last for ever; in reality, the couple were a lot poorer than their lifestyle indicated. But there was another, more sinister, reason why Bury might have wanted a change of address: if he was to murder his wife, he would need a secluded apartment where there were no neighbours who might hear sounds of a struggle. He could not attack his wife in the Robertsons' lodgings, because it is obvious that they would have heard Ellen screaming and would have intervened. Therefore, he may have engineered the row about the rent to give him the excuse he needed to leave.

And there was yet another reason why William Bury might have wanted to get away from the Robertsons' house. He had posted a letter to Margaret Corney giving 43 Union Street as his (and his wife's) address. If something happened to Ellen, there was the possibility that a letter might have arrived for her from Margaret Corney and that Mrs Robertson might have returned the letter with an explanation that Ellen was now dead. In such a situation, Margaret Corney would have been certain to go to the police. This hypothesis is supported by the fact that Margaret Corney did not receive a letter from Ellen informing her of their change of address. Bearing in mind that Ellen had promised to write again, it seems strange that, at the very least, she did not send her sister a quick note with her new address. It may well be that William and Ellen sat down together to write Margaret Corney a second letter from their new address and that William Bury promised to post it but destroyed the letter instead.

On the morning of 28 January, William Bury called at the offices of J. & E. Shepherd, House Agents of 20 Cowgate, Dundee. He spoke to a 38-year-old clerk called James Lynn and asked him if he had any two-roomed houses to let. Lynn gave him the key to a two-roomed basement flat at the bottom of a tenement at 113 Princes Street. Bury looked at the property but then returned with the key, handing it to Mr Lynn and saying only that the property needed some repairs.

At 11 a.m. on Tuesday, 29 January, William and Ellen Bury left the Robertson lodgings. William Bury returned shortly afterwards to pack the unlocked box with his clothing. He told Margaret Robertson that his wife had started a job and that he had also got a job and was to start next day. About noon, William Bury went back to J. & E. Shepherd and asked James Lynn for the key to the property in Princes Street so that his wife might view it. Lynn gave him the key but this time Bury did not return it.

At 1.30 p.m., two men arrived at Mrs Robertson's premises to collect the Burys' luggage. Margaret Robertson looked out of the window and saw William Bury in the street below standing next to a barrow which had a bed on it. She let the men take the luggage, which comprised two large wooden boxes or trunks. One of the boxes was very heavy. It was later reported that, as the men struggled with the boxes, one of them jocularly said, 'It's like as if there was a dead man in it.'

7

'JACK THE RIPPER IS QUIET, NOW'

THE TENEMENT IN PRINCES STREET THAT THE BURYS MOVED INTO was a four-storey building. Dwelling houses occupied the top two storeys while the ground floor, which was on street level, was taken up by shops. The tenement also had a basement and it was into this sunken area that the Burys moved on Tuesday, 29 January 1889.

The property had previously been used as a tailor's workshop. There were no furnishings and there was no grate in the fireplace. Princes Street was a tenemented street, meaning that there were high buildings on either side. It is unlikely that direct sunlight would ever have shone into the basement flat – even at noon in high summer. To make matters worse, the property was north-facing.

The rent was cheap at two shillings and sixpence per week. But William Bury was not interested even in paying such a small sum. Twice messengers were sent from J. & E. Shepherd to ask if the Burys intended to rent the property: they would knock on the door and peer in the window to no avail as the occupants refused to answer.

In the words of the *Dundee Advertiser*, the new house was 'very dingy' but it probably suited William Bury's purposes perfectly. Although it was in a populated area, the basement flats were separated from the flats above by a whole floor of shops. It was very unlikely that noises made in the basement would be heard upstairs. The only concern might have been the flats on either side because the walls were made of lath and plaster and were not completely soundproof.

We will never know what Ellen Bury thought of her new home. Her first view of it would have come as the couple walked up Princes Street amongst the hustle and bustle of commercial traffic: horses, carts and people going about their everyday business. There was a railing running along the inside edge of the pavement and the tenement was set back from the pavement with a moat-like drop between the tenement and the railing. The Burys went through a gate in the railing and down a stair to their flat.

The apartment was dirty: the front door and windows were covered in grime. The kitchen was empty and filthy. The other room was small and equally bare and had not even a grate in the fireplace. A window pane was broken, which means a cold draught was probably blowing through the apartment.

Ellen Bury was described by her sister Margaret as always 'very delicate'. Here she was, in winter, moving into a cold basement flat that did not receive any direct sunlight and did not have a grate in the fireplace.

The first person to speak to William Bury in Princes Street was Mrs Marjory Smith, who, along with her husband, worked in the shop directly above the Burys' flat. The Smiths were described as 'licensed brokers', which means either that they were pawnbrokers or that they bought and sold second-hand goods. On Monday, 28 January, Mrs Smith was standing at her shop door watching the comings and goings in the street when she saw William Bury walking up the street and looking about him a lot. He went over to Mrs Smith and asked her if she knew which of the houses was the one that was available to rent. Mrs Smith showed him down the stair to the sunken flat.

Marjory Smith next saw William Bury on Tuesday afternoon. He and his wife had been down to the Greenmarket that morning to buy some furniture for the empty flat. (The Greenmarket was an open-air fruit and vegetable market near the docks which also sold a lot of second-hand goods.) There, they had been able to buy a cheap iron bedstead and some bedclothing – and, for a few shillings, had also bought two chairs, several earthenware plates, two or three cups and saucers, a teapot and some china ornaments.

On Tuesday afternoon, Marjory Smith saw William Bury, assisted by two men, carrying the packing cases and the bed down the stairway. Shortly after 6 p.m., he came into her shop and asked if she had any pillows. She showed him some and he said that he would fetch his wife and let her see them. They returned soon afterwards and Ellen Bury bought two pillows, a flock bed, two half-mattresses and a candlestick.

This means that William and Ellen Bury could not have been sleeping together. By now they were clearly sleeping in separate beds. Curiously, however, the police found only the iron bedstead when they searched the flat two weeks later. By then, the flock bed had mysteriously disappeared.

Mrs Smith chatted to Ellen Bury as William Bury carried these items downstairs. Mrs Smith asked why they had left London and how William Bury was employed there. Ellen told her that he had had a pony and cart and had sold sawdust but that he had got mixed up in bad company and had stayed out late at night. She said she was glad to get him away from this 'bad company' to see if he would do any better.

When Bury returned, he said that the bed he had bought needed a spar. Mrs Smith's husband, Alexander, gave him one and went down with Bury to the flat below to help him fix the spar to the bed. When the two men came back, Mrs Smith invited Bury and his wife into her back shop. Bury immediately offered to go for beer and although Mrs Smith said she did not want any herself, she told Bury that he could get anything he wanted for himself and his wife.

Bury subsequently disappeared and then returned with a pot of beer. Mrs Smith spread the table with bread and butter but Ellen Bury did not eat much, preferring to drink a glass of beer. Bury himself drank a lot of beer. After some time, he offered his wife a second glass but she shook her head, remarking, 'Oh no, I've got enough. You know I don't take it.'

Mrs Smith noticed that William Bury 'partook freely of the liquor'. Her impression of Ellen Bury was that she was 'a very nice young person'. Mrs Smith said that Ellen Bury was genteelly dressed with an ulster and a nice hat and brown dress. She also said that Ellen Bury was taller than William Bury which appears to conflict with the evidence of Dr Templeman, who measured Ellen's dead body at 5 ft 1¼ in.

There is no explanation for this. William Bury's height was probably not measured by the City of Dundee Police. The hangman would have been more concerned with estimating Bury's weight and may not have measured his height. The

Dundee Advertiser published his height as 5 ft 3½ in. but it is not clear how the *Advertiser* got its information.

We do not know how or why Mrs Smith formed this opinion. If she was observing William and Ellen Bury while they were sitting at the table together, it is possible that she failed to take account of his body posture. If William Bury adopted a slouching posture, he may have appeared smaller than Ellen.

It is also worth bearing in mind that this was the only time Mrs Smith saw the Burys sitting or standing together. On the next occasion she saw them (when she went to retrieve a chopper), he was sitting but she was standing. Mrs Smith was not in the Burys' company often, and did not see them together regularly.

Mrs Smith noticed that William Bury was wearing a jet ring and a gold ring on his little fingers. She asked him about these and he replied proudly, 'These were my wedding gifts.'

Mrs Smith then asked Bury about his business and he replied that he was a sawdust merchant. Mrs Smith immediately voiced her disapproval. 'You were one of the men who goes about with a donkey cart and supplies sawdust to shops?'

'Yes,' Ellen Bury answered, defending her husband. 'He didn't have a donkey, he had a pony and very good money he made too.'

'He won't make much at that trade here,' Mrs Smith said.

William Bury seemed to admit as much himself. 'The Reverend Gough, the Episcopal minister,' he said, 'knows me well and will put me up to something.'

The conversation drifted on to other topics. Mrs Smith could not resist asking these Londoners about Jack the Ripper, saying, 'What sort of work was this you Whitechapel folk have been about, letting Jack the Ripper kill so many people?'

William Bury seemed to go silent at this point. But Ellen Bury made a very strange comment, remarking, 'Jack the Ripper is quiet, now.' Curiously, she is also reported to have said to another neighbour, 'Jack the Ripper is taking a rest.'

These are bizarre comments for Ellen to make: first, they imply knowledge of Jack the Ripper and, second, they are contradicted by many of the stories in the newspapers.

Only one week previously, the *Dundee Courier* had carried a report that Jack the Ripper had been responsible for the disappearance of two women in north-west Spain. The story might have been false, even ludicrous, but what is important about this is that the popular press was not creating the impression that Jack the Ripper was 'taking a rest'. So where did Ellen Bury get this idea?

What is disturbing about this is that her comment gives a good description of her own husband. The violent, argumentative wife-beater was now spending quiet evenings indoors with his wife. William Bury did seem to have 'gone quiet'.

Could Ellen Bury have suspected her husband of being Jack the Ripper? Surely she would not have continued to live with him if she did so. But she had so far continued to live with William Bury even though he had stolen her money, attempted to kill her, frequently assaulted her and given her a venereal disease. It is hard to imagine what William Bury might have done to make Ellen leave him. Somehow, Ellen Bury got the idea that Jack the Ripper had 'gone quiet'. The only thing we can say for certain is that she did *not* get that idea from the popular press.

We will never know what passed between the Burys in private conversation. But we do know that William Bury was a heavy drinker. Could he have let slip things about Jack the Ripper in drunken conversation?

William Bury was back in the Smiths' shop the following day when he bought a kettle and some crockery. Two days later, on 1 February, he was back in the shop again to buy a goblet, some plates and a fender. He also asked Mrs Smith if she had a grate for sale. She told him that she did not but was able to offer him instead the ribs of a grate.

If Mrs Smith's witness statement is accurate, it means that the Burys lived in the basement flat from Tuesday to Friday without a fire. This seems extraordinary when we consider that it was January/February, that there was a broken window pane and that they had a basement flat, meaning that no heat came up from flats below.

Mrs Smith also stated that, later that same day, William Bury came back and asked her if she would lend him a chopper. She did so and as he was leaving, he put the chopper over his shoulder. At this point, Mrs Smith said, 'Surely you are not Jack the Ripper?'

Presumably the comment was meant to be a joke. Bury, however, did not treat it as one. In a guarded reply which may have indicated edginess, he said, 'I do not know so much about that,' and then left.

The next day was Saturday, 2 February. By early evening, William Bury still had not returned the chopper. Mrs Smith decided she had waited long enough and went downstairs herself to get it back. She found the Burys taking tea in the back room. William Bury was already much the worse for drink. Ellen Bury, who was sober, gave Mrs Smith the chopper. This was the last time that Mrs Smith saw Ellen Bury alive.

When the Burys first moved into Princes Street, Ellen Bury seemed to despair of her husband's feeble efforts to get a job and took one herself. She was employed as a sweeper with Baxter Brothers – one of the biggest linen and jute spinning and weaving firms in Dundee – but worked there for only one day. Bury met her at the main gate during her dinner hour and in the open street – as the *Courier* was to say – 'he took her round the neck and kissed her, as the English folk do'. He then took her to the Prince Regent Bar in Princes Street, where they had some beer and bread for their dinner.

When Mrs Smith saw Mrs Bury next, she told her that it was not the custom in Scotland for women to go openly into public houses and that she had better not do it again. 'Oh, indeed, the women of Scotland will drink on the sly,' Ellen replied. The following day, Mrs Smith asked Bury about his wife when he called into her shop. Bury said, 'She does not feel very well, she don't like that kind of work and I don't think she will go back.'

This statement of Bury's does have the ring of truth. Ellen was a frail woman who was probably unsuited to the hard physical work that was expected of the women who worked in the jute mills. However, it is possible that she had worked in a jute mill before. Margaret Corney said so at the trial. Unfortunately, Corney refused to say that her sister was a prostitute, which casts some doubt on her evidence. Nevertheless, it may be the case that Ellen had worked in a mill before she went into prostitution. Therefore, she may have known what she was letting herself in for.

The most likely explanation for Ellen Bury's decision not to go back to work at Baxter's was that it did not fit in with William Bury's plans. In fact, her decision to get a job was a serious impediment to his plan to murder her. Baxter's employed people to go around and knock on the windows of their workers to wake them up early in the mornings. Such a person was called the 'chapper-up'.

If Ellen continued to work at the mill, the chapper-up was going to come round every morning to knock on the window. More worrying than that was the risk that someone from Baxter Brothers might come round to Bury's house to ask why his wife was not at work, when her corpse had newly been squeezed into a box in the back room.

Another shopkeeper who had some dealings with William Bury was Janet Martin. Mrs Martin was a provision merchant, or grocer, who had a shop a few doors along from Bury's house. On the day that Bury moved into the Princes Street property, he went to Mrs Martin's shop and asked if she had any firewood. At first, she did not understand his English accent and thought he was selling firewood. 'Oh no,' Bury told her, 'I want to buy some wood.'

'I am sorry to say I have none at present,' was Mrs Martin's reply.

Bury then asked her if she had any candles. She took one from the shelf and offered it to him. 'How much is that?' Bury asked.

'A penny, please,' Mrs Martin said.

'A penny!' Bury exclaimed. 'Do you know I would get three for a penny in London?'

'Then it's a pity you did not bring them with you,' Mrs Martin replied, perhaps jokingly, 'but I'll give you two for three halfpence.' Bury took two and paid. He came to her shop nearly every day after that to buy candles, matches, firewood and sometimes bread.

One day when Bury was buying bread, Mrs Martin offered him a stale loaf for fivepence halfpenny. Bury reacted in the usual manner, saying, 'Oh, my, fivepence halfpenny. Why I could get five old loaves in the East End of London for that.' Mrs Martin, however, would not let him beat her down on the price. 'Well, you'd better go to the baker up the street and see what he will charge,' she said.

One thing Mrs Martin noticed was the furtive way William Bury looked about him. He could not look a person in the face and, if he realised someone was looking at him, usually dropped his eyes. The last time that Mrs Martin saw Bury was on Saturday, 9 February when he asked for some candles and matches. After she had served him, he said in his normal brusque manner, 'Oh, I'll pay you tomorrow.'

'Na, na,' Mrs Martin said. 'Tomorrow's not ours.'

As Bury paid the money, Mrs Martin noticed that the jet ring was broken and only half of it was left on his finger. But it was only when the news of the murder broke in the newspapers three days later that Mrs Martin would realise that he had actually purchased the murder weapon – a length of cord – in her shop. She may also have come to realise that the ring must have been broken by Ellen Bury fighting for her life.

The only neighbour who saw much of either Bury or his wife was Mrs Mary Lee, who lived next door with her husband. Like the Burys, the Lees also lived in a basement flat. Mrs Lee often passed William Bury on the stairs and thought him a quiet, modest man. She knew that the property had no grate when he moved in and asked Bury if he was going to put a woman in there without a grate. Bury, who seems to have had a lie for every occasion, told her that the landlord would be putting in a grate.

Mrs Lee described Ellen Bury as a thin, delicate-looking woman but could hardly understand a word she said because 'she was so English'. Mrs Lee saw Ellen Bury only rarely and never found out her first name. Nevertheless, she described her as a 'quiet-looking woman . . . neatly dressed, generally wearing an ulster and a bonnet'.

Mrs Lee described Ellen as wearing her hair up with a fringe. She said that Mrs Bury never seemed to go out of the house except sometimes at night when she would go out into the street to draw water from the communal pump or well. (At that time, there were both communal pumps and wells in Princes Street.) Mrs Lee noticed that William Bury was in the habit of running all the errands. Although she did not say so, Mrs Lee must have been in the habit of looking through the Burys' front window whenever she passed because she stated that she had never even seen Ellen Bury walking across the floor.

If Ellen Bury was not going out of the house and not walking about within the house, what was she doing? She may have been lying in bed for long periods – particularly if she had a weak constitution and it was a poorly heated house. It is hard to imagine what else she might have been doing.

The first two mornings after the Burys came to live next door to the Lees, they were 'knocked up' by a boy. Mrs Lee took this to be an indication that they were employed in a jute mill somewhere in the city. The knocking up soon stopped and Ellen Bury was only rarely seen out and about after that.

William Bury regularly went out at eight o'clock in the morning (when the Prince Regent Bar in Princes Street opened each day). He often passed Mrs Lee as he was entering or leaving the house but seldom spoke to her. By now, it was obvious that William Bury was going for all their messages. Mrs Lee also noticed that William Bury usually left his house door open when he went out during his first week in Princes Street; but, for some reason, Bury always took the precaution of closing it during his second week there. Nobody seemed to ask why Bury was locking his door if his wife was alive and well and living in the house.

Another odd thing about the Burys was that Mr and Mrs Lee never heard them doing anything. This was unusual, if not peculiar, because the Lees had heard the previous tenants of No. 113 moving about. On Tuesday, 5 February, late in the evening, Mrs Lee was at the back of the tenement when she saw there were no lights on in the Burys' window. Everything was eerily quiet and Mrs Lee joked to her husband, 'These folks are surely dead.'

The house in Princes Street had almost become a prison for Ellen Bury, so rarely was she seen out of doors. The house had inadequate furnishings and Ellen and her husband did not converse much, if at all. She did not read, which leads us to wonder how she might have occupied her time in a dingy flat for 12 or more hours each day. It is possible she spent a lot of the time in bed because she was a weak woman experiencing the colder Scottish climate for the first time and doing so in winter in an inadequately heated house.

In the meantime, William Bury made no effort to look for work but kept up his drinking habits. The nearest public house, the Prince Regent Bar at 129 Princes Street, was owned by Alexander Patterson. According to Patterson, Bury was in his public house 'usually once or twice a day'. While Mrs Robertson and Mrs Lee had found Bury a very taciturn man, he was exactly the opposite to the locals in the Prince Regent Bar and seemed happy to converse with anyone in the bar. Alexander Patterson could only remember Bury bringing his wife with him on one occasion, when she had half a glass of port wine. It appeared to Patterson that Bury was 'very kind' to his wife. Although Bury usually seemed talkative in the bar, he never revealed much about his private life.

Sometimes Bury would stay and drink in the Prince Regent Bar but more often than not he would take a glass of beer back to his flat and then return an hour or two later for another glass. He always had plenty of money to pay his way and never asked for anything 'on tick'. Anyone who struck up a conversation with Bury was likely to be offered a drink but Bury would never allow them to buy him a beer in return.

But Bury, by this time, was acting out a role. In the days after his wife's death, he would talk about her in the Prince Regent Bar as if they were happily married. He was often heard to remark that his 'old woman' would need something for her supper and would carry away a bottle of beer which was allegedly for her but which in fact he was going to be drinking himself.

The only person to make friends with William Bury was David Walker, a painter who was repainting the inside and outside of the Prince Regent Bar at this time. Bury was such a regular customer that the men got into conversation on several occasions. They were both the same age but, whatever the reason, developed a liking for each other. Walker stated vaguely that their conversations were on 'general subjects'.

David Walker saw Ellen Bury twice in the last week of her life. The first occasion was on Saturday, 2 February, when he saw the couple in Princes Street. The second occasion was on Monday, 4 February, when he saw her walking down King Street towards the city centre (King Street led off Princes Street). Ellen Bury was wearing a tweed suit. This picture of her walking into town with her husband is the last one we have of her.

In the days that followed, none of the neighbours seemed to notice that Ellen Bury stopped going out of her house at night to fetch water. Nor did they think to question why the blind was drawn down over the Burys' back window on Tuesday, 5 February, and remained drawn all week.

8

A WOMAN SCREAMING

ON MONDAY, 4 FEBRUARY, WILLIAM BURY HAD WALKED INTO Janet Martin's shop and said, 'Can you give me a piece of cord, please?'

Mrs Martin could not remember if his visit took place in the forenoon or afternoon but she did clearly remember opening a drawer in the counter and handing him a length of rope, the type of which was generally used for roping boxes.

The rope was rolled up but Bury unravelled it in front of the shopkeeper and examined it carefully. While he was looking at it, Mrs Martin remarked that she would fetch him another rope if that one would not do.

Bury replied, 'This will do nicely, thank you,' and left without saying what the rope was required for.

David Duncan, a 44-year-old labourer, lived with his landlady at 101 Princes Street. His back window was 29 yards from the Burys' back window. Duncan had gone to bed between 10 p.m. and 11 p.m. on Monday, 4 February.

Early on Tuesday morning, Duncan woke up. It was dark and Duncan reckoned that he must have been asleep for two or three hours because the coal fire, which had been burning brightly when he went to bed, had gone out.

'Having reason to rise out of bed, I did so,' Duncan stated. Presumably he meant that he needed to relieve himself, although this was never properly explained. While he was standing on the floor, he heard a woman screaming in terror. He could not make out what she was saying. The screaming stopped almost as abruptly as it had begun. Duncan immediately woke up his landlady, Ann Johnstone, and said, 'Do you hear that, Annie – a woman screaming?'

Forty-six-year-old Ann Johnstone listened for a few moments and then answered, 'No.' Then the two of them listened together for a while longer but heard nothing more. Duncan later stated, 'I am quite certain that the sound of the female screaming came from the direction of Bury's house.'

One of the more comical moments at the trial was the evidence of Francis Duffy, shoemaker, who lived at 109 Princes Street with his wife Susan. They both testified that they heard no sounds of screaming on the night of the murder. Francis Duffy had both a shop and a backshop, and he and his wife used the backshop as a dwelling house. Their backshop was situated above the Burys' flat.

Francis Duffy's statement ran as follows:

> The first and indeed the only time I ever saw this man [i.e. Bury] was one day at dinner time, between 2 p.m. and 3 p.m., cleaning his front window. If it had not been for seeing the accused then, I would not have known there was any person living below, as I had heard neither before nor after the least noise of any one moving in the house below.
>
> We usually go to bed at about twelve o'clock at night and so far as I could say we went to bed at that hour on the night when Mrs Bury is said to have been killed.
>
> I did not hear any noise or cry during that night and think if she had cried I would likely have heard it.

Francis Duffy was one of the defence witnesses and his statement was used by the Defence in an attempt to rebut the prosecution allegation that Mrs Bury had been murdered. However, his credibility was destroyed when he admitted:

> I was in my own house during the evening and night of Sunday, 10 February, when the detectives had been recovering Mrs Bury's body and neither heard any movement in Bury's house or knew anything of what had taken place until next morning. It is therefore possible for a good deal to be done in Bury's house without any sound of it reaching our house.

For Francis Duffy to be called as a defence witness showed up the extreme poverty of the defence case.

From Tuesday, 5 February onwards, William Bury went to the Prince Regent Bar more and more frequently. He was in the public house for his breakfast at 9 a.m. on Tuesday morning. David Walker noticed that Bury was wearing a dark suit with a brown top coat and seemed quite sober.

Sometime during the week that followed, Bury went back to Mrs Jane Robertson's lodgings and asked if there was any mail for him from London. He seemed disappointed when she told him that nothing had come for him. He had no correspondence and now found himself with no money and no means of getting out of Dundee. He also had to decide how he was going to dispose of the body in his flat.

Between Tuesday, 5 February and Saturday, 9 February, Bury was in the Prince Regent Bar several times a day. It was during this time that his friendship with David Walker developed. Walker was in Bury's company until 11 p.m. on Saturday night when he left him at the top of the stair that led down to his house. According to Walker, Bury was 'a little under the influence of liquor but spoke quite sensibly'.

The following day was Sunday, 10 February. Walker was in bed about noon when he was surprised to be visited by William Bury. They exchanged a few words and then Walker handed Bury a copy of the *People's Journal*, which he had been reading as he lay in bed. Bury read aloud a paragraph about an elopement which had ended in suicide. Then a strange thing happened.

Walker said, 'Never mind about the elopements and suicides, look to see if there is anything about Jack the Ripper, you that knows the place.'

Bury seemed to get the fright of his life and immediately threw down the newspaper. Did he respond like this because he was Jack the Ripper? Or was he jumpy because he had murdered his wife?

If the only murder William Bury committed was the murder of his wife, it remains a fact that he was able to sleep in his house with her body packed into a box by his bed for six consecutive nights. During this time, he was going into the Prince Regent Bar every day and talking to people about his wife as if she was still alive. The evidence that we have suggests that the murder of his wife had *not* made William Bury jumpy. Nevertheless, we should not completely discount it as a possible explanation.

Therefore we have three possible explanations:

- he got a fright because he was Jack the Ripper;
- he got a fright because he was a murderer, though not necessarily Jack the Ripper;
- this was a Sunday and Bury was on edge because he had not been able to get anything to drink.

Coincidentally, another Englishman lived at the top of Walker's stair. On hearing either him or his wife rattle some pots and pans, Walker remarked that the English people fed themselves well on Sundays. Bury agreed, replying, 'If my Mrs and I had not a good dinner on Sunday we would think ourselves not right.'

Walker now jokingly asked Bury if he was having a turkey for dinner. Bury seems to have taken the question seriously, answering, 'No, my missus has a rabbit and a piece of pork, and she had told me to hurry home at 1.30 p.m. or I would miss my chance.' Bury duly left Walker's house at about 1.30 p.m. and returned one hour afterwards. (Walker's address of 19 Crescent Lane was between 200 and 300 yards from Bury's house.)

When he returned, Bury suggested that they might go for a walk. Walker agreed and the two men went for a walk by the shore till about 5 p.m. By 'the shore', Walker probably meant the docks, which were only a short distance from Princes Street. As they walked together, Bury told Walker that marriage was 'a bother and a trouble'. He then asked Walker if ships sailed from Dundee to Hull, Glasgow and Liverpool and added, confusingly, that he had a good mind to go back to London to see his old pals. But if Bury was thinking about going to London, why was he asking about boats to Liverpool, Glasgow and Hull?

Walker's statement ends with the comment that Bury 'appeared to be very restless in his manner but spoke quite sensibly and was quite sober'. But perhaps the most interesting part of the statement is a note scribbled in the margin and signed, mysteriously, 'A. A.' which reads, 'This witness gave his statement with considerable reluctance and I believe if pressed will say Bury gave him to understand he was tired of married life.'

Two hours after he parted company with Walker, Bury walked into the Central Police Station in West Bell Street, Dundee, and told Lieutenant Parr that he had woken up to find his wife dead on the floor.

There is one thing about the murder of Ellen Bury that seems contradictory. It appears to have been planned: William Bury forged a contract of employment with a jute spinner in Dundee so that he could get Ellen Bury away from London. If he had murdered her in London, a string of witnesses would have come forward to tell the police that he had been repeatedly violent towards her (Elizabeth Haynes, Margaret Corney, William Smith and James Martin).

Bury therefore took her to Dundee and was careful, while in the city, to create a new image for himself. Although he was still drinking, he was now quiet in the company of his wife. Witnesses like Margaret Robertson testified that she thought them a happily married couple. Bury was also doing all the shopping: shopkeepers like Janet Martin and Marjory Smith testified that it was always William Bury who was coming into their shops and doing the messages, never his wife.

Up to the point at which the murder was committed, Bury had gone to a lot of trouble to create a new image of himself. In fact, nothing he did while he was in Dundee suggested to anyone that he might have been a murderer.

But the plan broke down once the murder had been committed. Bury seems to have thought everything out – up to that point. Then he seems to have had no idea what to do next. Absolutely no thought went into his escape from Dundee.

Once the murder had been carried out, Bury had two problems. The first was that representatives of J. & E. Shepherd, House Agents, were going to continue visiting the property at 113 Princes Street to try to gain access. The second was that neighbours and shopkeepers in the surrounding area would never see Ellen Bury again and might eventually ask what had happened to her.

Bury could not leave Dundee until he had disposed of the body because the body would have been discovered and the police would have begun to conduct a search for him. But he does not seem to have put any thought into the disposal of the body before the murder. He packed it into the case that he had asked William Smith to make. But then he left it in his back room as if he did not know what else to do.

Jack the Ripper had never had to dispose of a body because he always fled the scene of the crime. Jack the Ripper's modus operandi was to identify a victim and kill her by means of strangulation followed by mutilation of the body with a knife. There appeared to be no motive beyond sadistic pleasure. Then he would flee before any witnesses came upon the scene. When Jack the Ripper committed a murder, he never needed to go beyond the execution of the crime itself.

In William Bury's case, the scene of the crime became incriminating because it was the house in which he lived. Bury does not seem to have thought about this until it was too late. Jack the Ripper did not have to think about disposing of the body or disguising the fact that there had been a murder. It is clear that William Bury did not think about disposing of the body or hiding the fact that there had been a murder.

Bury's motive was not money because he had already got access to all of his wife's money. His only motive seems to be that of sadistic pleasure. Death was caused by strangulation followed by mutilation of the body with a knife. In other words, the modus operandi was very similar to that of Jack the Ripper.

9

THE TRIAL BEGINS

THE SPRING CIRCUIT COURT OF FORFARSHIRE OPENED IN Dundee on Thursday, 28 March, when Lord Young took his seat on the bench a few minutes before 10 a.m.

George, Lord Young had travelled up from Edinburgh on Wednesday by the Caledonian train, arriving at 9.40 p.m., and had stayed overnight at the Queen's Hotel. He was 69 years old and earlier in his career had been a junior counsel at the celebrated trial of Madeleine Smith for the murder of Emile L'Angelier (30 June–8 July 1857). It was later said that Madeleine Smith owed her acquittal to George Young's skill in preparing her defence. According to the *Dictionary of National Biography*, Lord Young 'particularly excelled in the severe cross-examination of hostile witnesses'. He accepted a judgeship in 1874 and took his seat on the bench of the Court of Session with the title of Lord Young.

The court house was crowded; hundreds of people congregated in front of the Town House like spectators at a football match and a considerable crowd remained there all day. The Reverend R.S. Warren, of St David's Parish Church, began proceedings with a prayer. As soon as he was finished, Bury was brought into the courtroom. The spectators in the public gallery were probably never more quiet than they were at the moment when Bury, dressed in a dark suit and carrying a tweed overcoat on his arm and a felt hat in his hand, took his place in the dock. His hair was combed and his whiskers neatly trimmed.

The charge was read out: 'William Henry Bury, prisoner in the

Prison of Dundee, you are indicted at the instance of the Right Honourable James Patrick Bannerman Robertson, Her Majesty's Advocate, and the charge against you is that on 5 February 1889, in the dwelling house occupied by you in Princes Street, Dundee, you did strike, stab and strangle Ellen Bury, your wife, and did murder her.'

Lord Young now addressed William Bury. 'William Henry Bury, you are charged with the crime of murder. Are you guilty or not guilty?'

Bury replied, 'Not guilty, my Lord,' but the *Dundee Advertiser* reported that he looked somewhat concerned and sat in the dock with his arms folded. It was not long, however, before Bury was giving the impression that he was the least concerned person in the entire court. He occasionally listened attentively but for most of the time his eyes wandered about the court. It was only when the prosecuting and defence counsel began their initial addresses to the jury that he showed an interest in the trial. For most of the time, his face was a mask from which nothing could be read.

The Prosecution was led by 44-year-old Dugald McKechnie, the son of a farmer from the Isle of Jura. McKechnie trotted out a long list of prosecution witnesses, including Margaret Corney, Elizabeth Haynes, James Martin and William Smith. If Bury had hoped to escape their damaging testimonies by relocating to Dundee, he was badly mistaken.

Bury had employed as his defence counsel a local solicitor called David James Tweedie. But Tweedie did not defend Bury himself. Instead, he brought in a sharp-witted advocate called William Hay. Hay was the son of a town clerk of Dundee and was 30 years old. He would give the Prosecution a run for their money and nearly got his client off the hook.

The trial proper started with the evidence of Dr Templeman. The only 'witness' to the murder was David Duncan, who heard a woman screaming and judged that the screams came from the direction of the Burys' house. The only other evidence that a murder had occurred came from the medical evidence. Drs Templeman and Stalker had examined the body on the night of 10/11 February and concluded that Ellen Bury could not have inflicted the injuries upon herself and that the cause of death had to be murder. The police sought a third opinion. Dr Henry Duncan Littlejohn, the police surgeon in Edinburgh, was summoned to Dundee, where he also conducted a post-mortem examination. He concurred with Templeman and Stalker's findings.

In the witness box, Dr Littlejohn gave a succinct description of Ellen Bury's last moments:

> LORD YOUNG: Give us in detail your opinion of the case in all its medical aspects.
>
> DR LITTLEJOHN: My opinion is that a struggle having taken place, a blow was struck on the left temporal muscle.
>
> LORD YOUNG: Is that the bruise which Dr Templeman said was more likely to have been caused by a stick or a poker?
>
> DR LITTLEJOHN: That is the one, my Lord. It is in a concealed part of the head. It is in a hollow and not so likely, therefore, to have been caused by a fall – the other and more prominent parts of the head being more likely under these circumstances to suffer. The blow was, in my opinion, sufficiently strong to render the deceased either unconscious or semi-unconscious. The application of the ligature to the neck followed, producing suffocation; and while the deceased was moribund the various wounds described in the medical report were inflicted.

The three medical men were therefore very consistent in their analysis. But that did not stop Hay going on the attack when Dr Templeman went into the witness box.

> HAY: You have described in your report a mark at the back of the left ear and one on the left shoulder. Are you aware that these marks disappeared when washed by Dr Lennox on 14 February?
>
> DR TEMPLEMAN: I would be very much surprised to hear it.
>
> HAY: There are two wounds below the jaw described. Would you be surprised to hear that on the 14th they also disappeared on the application of a wet towel?
>
> DR TEMPLEMAN: I would.
>
> LORD YOUNG: Would you be surprised to hear that what you had taken to be bruises was blood? (LAUGHTER)
>
> HAY: In your report, you say there was an incised wound on the nose. Might not the cause which made that wound also have caused the blow on the eyebrow at the same time?

DR TEMPLEMAN: Very possibly.

HAY: And that may have been the result of a fall?

DR TEMPLEMAN: Quite possible.

HAY: Did you make any examination of this woman's stomach to find traces of alcohol?

DR TEMPLEMAN: No, except the sense of smell, and there was no smell of alcohol.

LORD YOUNG: Was the stomach empty?

DR TEMPLEMAN: There was some partially digested food in the stomach.

HAY: Are you aware that the odour of alcohol rapidly disappears from a dead body?

DR TEMPLEMAN: Yes.

HAY: And that there is no other means of ascertaining it other than by medical tests?

DR TEMPLEMAN: Yes.

HAY: Why did you not apply that test here?

DR TEMPLEMAN: Because the cause of death was very apparent. No poison could have produced the condition of the body in which we found it.

HAY: I refer you to the second volume of Taylor on Medical Jurisprudence, page 75, where it is stated, 'Before a charge of murder by strangulation is raised against any person from marks of violence found on a dead body, care should be taken that they admit of no other probable explanation other than the direct application of violence.' Do you accept that?

DR TEMPLEMAN: Yes.

HAY: Did you examine the feet of this dead woman?

DR TEMPLEMAN: Yes.

HAY: Was there any blood on the feet?

DR TEMPLEMAN: No.

HAY: I think the feet were very dirty?

DR TEMPLEMAN: Yes; they had not been washed for a considerable period.

LORD YOUNG: You did not take that for bruises, did you?
(LAUGHTER)

Hay's strategy was obviously to create enough room for doubt in the minds of the jury. If it was at all possible that Bury's version of events could have occurred then the jury would be unable to convict. The absence of witnesses meant that the medical evidence had to be unambiguous.

Hay was trying to establish that it was possible that William Bury's version of events could have occurred, i.e. that Ellen Bury had been drinking and had attempted to strangle herself in the night during the course of which she lost consciousness and fell, thus sustaining injuries to the head. Hay continued this line of questioning when he cross-examined Dr Littlejohn.

> McKECHNIE: You have heard what was said in the report as to the everted character of these wounds. What does that indicate in your opinion?
>
> DR LITTLEJOHN: As a rule, that points to the presence of life. Life does not leave the body after the circulation and respiration have stopped, and does not leave the body for an hour or so.
>
> McKECHNIE: Suppose Drs Templeman and Stalker saw this eversion of wounds on 11 February, and Drs Lennox and Kinnear [saw none] on the 14th, can you explain that away?
>
> DR LITTLEJOHN: The skin loses its flaccidity, owing to the advance of putrefaction, and all traces of it would be lost so that after ten days you might not see the eversion.
>
> HAY: What causes the disappearance of the everted edges?
>
> DR LITTLEJOHN: The elasticity of the skin disappears during the advance of the putrefactive process.
>
> HAY: The putrefactive process is shown by the discoloration of the skin?
>
> DR LITTLEJOHN: Not at all.
>
> HAY: You have seen many strange cases of suicide. Is this an unlikely case? A person puts a knot round the neck; the knot is at the left-hand side?
>
> DR LITTLEJOHN: You can't put a knot round the neck. (LAUGHTER)
>
> HAY: She pulls the knot tight, insensibility follows, and she tumbles to the ground on the top of the rope. Would that mean strangulation?
>
> DR LITTLEJOHN: The whole thing is highly improbable.
>
> HAY: A large amount of pressure is not demanded to produce unconsciousness?
>
> DR LITTLEJOHN: No, a very slight pressure produces unconsciousness.

HAY: Could the wound on the temporal muscle have been
   produced by a fall on the back of a chair?
DR LITTLEJOHN: I think it most unlikely.
HAY: Could it have been produced was my question?
DR LITTLEJOHN: It is quite possible.

Hay seemed to be making some ground here but the last word
went to McKechnie, the Advocate-Depute.

McKECHNIE: You know what the external symptoms of
   strangulation are. Are they all present in this case?
DR LITTLEJOHN: They are all very well marked in this case. It
   is a typical case, in my opinion, of homicidal strangulation.

McKechnie, the Advocate-Depute, had concluded his case. It was
5.58 p.m.
   Despite all Hay's efforts, he seemed to have lost the argument.
But Hay's trump card was the two doctors he had found who
would state on oath that, in their opinion, Ellen Bury had
committed suicide.

10

THE CASE FOR THE DEFENCE

THE COURTROOM WAS LIT BY TWO GAS JETS. AS IT GREW DARKER in the late afternoon and early evening, two candles were lit and placed on the bench. The overcrowded court was stiflingly warm but the dimness of the light gave the place a weird and shadowy appearance. The case for the Defence began when the Clerk of the Court read out William Bury's declaration.

> At Dundee, the eleventh day of February, 1889 years. In the presence of John Campbell Smith, Esquire, advocate, Sheriff-Substitute of Forfarshire, compeared a prisoner, also David James Tweedie, solicitor in Dundee, his agent, and the charge against the prisoner having been read over and explained to him, and he having been judicially admonished and examined there-anent, declares as follows: 'My name is William Henry Bury. I am 29 years, a sawdust merchant, and reside in Princes Street, Dundee. I simply deny the charge of murder made against me. I do not want to make any statement whatever either to the time or manner of her death. All which is truth. Signed William Henry Bury, J.C. Smith.'

Five witnesses appeared for the Defence. The first was the Reverend Gough, who had very little to say beyond the fact that William and Ellen Bury had attended one of his evening services and had spoken to him afterwards and that William Bury had asked him to help him get a job in Dundee. Two neighbours

(Susan Duffy and Jessie Gibson) were called to say that they heard no noises of a struggle on the night when Ellen Bury died but they also admitted that they heard no noises on Sunday, 10 February, when the body was taken away.

At this point, the defence case was looking shaky. Then came Hay's attempt to rebut the medical evidence. He called two local doctors as witnesses.

First to take the stand was Dr Lennox, who had been in practice for nine years. Lennox explained that he took the view that the case was one of suicide, not homicide, because:

- there were only three bruises, one on the nose and two on the anterior belly wall, and these might have been accidental;
- in homicidal strangulation it was almost inconceivable that there should be no marks on the neck except that made by the rope;
- suicide by strangulation was possible and could occur.

Lord Young challenged Dr Lennox, saying, 'Suicide by strangulation is possible and has occurred?'

Dr Lennox did not cite any examples where suicide by strangulation had occurred but nevertheless replied with a definite, 'Yes.' Lennox went on to give his opinion that the wounds on the body were inflicted *after* death and he stated on oath that there was no bruising on the left temporal muscle. At this point, Lord Young intervened again.

> LORD YOUNG: The difference is this. Drs Templeman and Stalker swear that when they examined the body on the 11 February there was eversion. You made your examination on the 14th, and you say you did not see eversion. Dr Littlejohn says that in his opinion, and according to his experience, the eversion would disappear in the interval. Do you differ or agree with him?
>
> DR LENNOX: I agree that marks of eversion if present might disappear in the interval.
>
> LORD YOUNG: Then that accounts for the whole of it, doesn't it?
>
> DR LENNOX: No, my Lord.
>
> LORD YOUNG: Drs Templeman and Stalker swear that when they examined the body on the 11 February there was eversion. You made your examination on the 14th and

you say you did not see eversion. Dr Littlejohn says that in his opinion, and according to his experience, the eversion would disappear in the interval. Do you agree with that?

DR LENNOX: I agree if there had been eversion that it might disappear in the interval.

LORD YOUNG: Then that accounts for the whole thing, Doctor. (LAUGHTER)

Dr Lennox justified his position by quoting authorities for the theory that in the circumstances there could not have been any eversion, and that eversion in any case must have disappeared before the green discoloration on the belly walls described by Drs Templeman and Stalker.

Dr Lennox had proved to be a stubborn witness for the Defence. Next into the witness box was Dr Kinnear. Coaxed by William Hay, Dr Kinnear said that he substantially agreed with what Dr Lennox had said. However, under cross-examination, Kinnear did not prove to be as strong a performer in the witness box as Lennox had been.

McKECHNIE: You are a graduate of a year?

DR KINNEAR: Yes.

McKECHNIE: Of less than six months?

DR KINNEAR: Yes.

McKECHNIE: You will get older, you know. (LAUGHTER).

LORD YOUNG: Is suicide by strangulation, unlike suicide by hanging, very rare?

DR KINNEAR: Very rare.

LORD YOUNG: If a woman was with her husband in bed of course he could strangle her without her making very much resistance?

DR KINNEAR: I think it is improbable, my Lord.

LORD YOUNG: Yes, of course, it is improbable that a husband will strangle his wife in any circumstances (LAUGHTER). So far as your knowledge goes, do you say that a case of suicide of this kind is unprecedented?

DR KINNEAR: It is, my Lord.

LORD YOUNG: That is very much what Dr Littlejohn said.

The case for the Defence was concluded at 7.05 p.m., having

occupied the court for only one hour. Lord Young told the jury that they could proceed with the trial or wait until next day. But if they decided to wait till next day, they would have to be kept in the custody of a macer, or court official, all night. The jurors decided to go on with the trial.

McKechnie, the Advocate-Depute, was first to address the jury. He put forward the argument that Bury had come to Scotland to commit murder because he thought it the wild land depicted in the novels of Walter Scott, where murders occurred daily without anyone noticing. He stressed that the only question in this case was whether the unfortunate woman committed suicide and whether the ghastly, horrible and brutal wounds were inflicted in a mad manner after her death. McKechnie attempted to ridicule the evidence of Dr Lennox, describing him more than once as the 'grandiloquent' Dr Lennox. He had listened to lectures from platforms and speeches from the Bar, he said, but he had never come across anyone as grandiloquent as Dr Lennox. Subsequent events would show this ridiculing of Lennox by McKechnie was a tactical mistake. If, McKechnie concluded, the jury was satisfied that the dead woman did not commit suicide, then her death lay at the prisoner's door.

Hay followed with his address to the jury. He argued that on the fatal evening, the deceased had been drinking and that she sustained her injuries when she fell down the stair leading to her home. He suggested that she had fallen on her left-hand side and went on to say that it was surely remarkable that all her injuries were sustained on her left-hand side. He held that suicide by strangulation was easy and said he cared not one jot for the medical evidence. He argued that a rope of the thickness and roughness produced in court would maintain its pressure if made into a slip knot, pulled tight and suddenly let go. Finally, Hay concluded that Bury, if guilty, had had the time to make his escape because he could have paid a fortnight's rent and been in the wildest parts of America by the time the body was discovered.

It was to become clear that Hay had won the battle of the lawyers. McKechnie's personal attack on Dr Lennox lost him the sympathy of the judge and perhaps also of some of the jurors. Meanwhile, Hay's more logical presentation had antagonised no one.

In summing up, Lord Young said that the only question before the jury was whether this was a case of suicide or murder. He

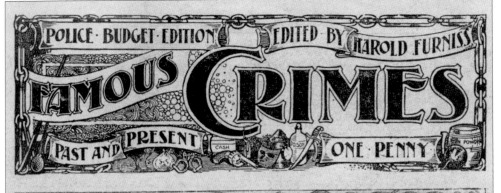

POLICE · BUDGET · EDITION   EDITED · BY HAROLD · FURNISS

FAMOUS CRIMES

PAST AND PRESENT   ONE · PENNY

HOW THE "RIPPER'S" VICTIMS WENT TO THEIR DEATH.

Vol. II.—No. 17.

A newspaper illustration shows how victims were allegedly lured to their deaths.

The back of the Hanbury Street building where Annie Chapman was found between the steps and the fence.

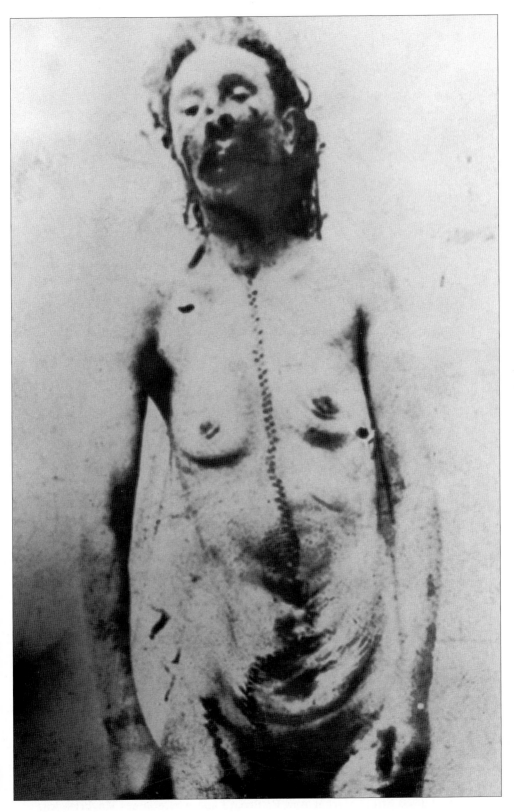

The mutilated body of Catherine Eddowes.

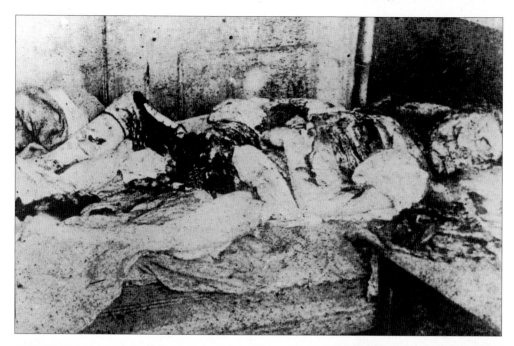

Top: A crime-scene photograph of Mary Kelly.

Bottom: Middlesex Street Market, now Petticoat Lane, where James Maybrick was reputed to have once rented a room.

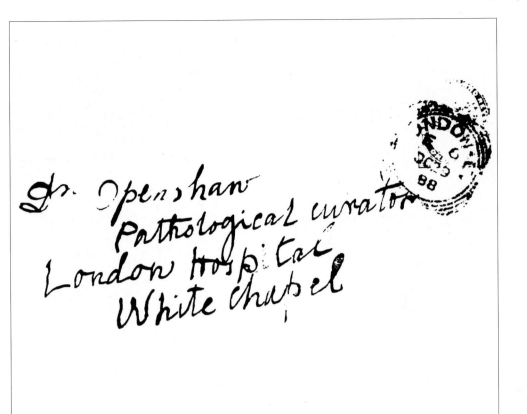

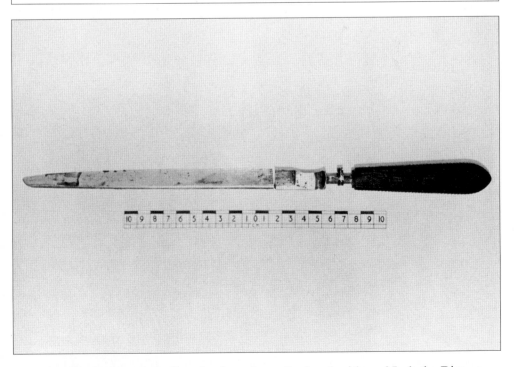

An example of what was believed to have been the handwriting of Jack the Ripper (*top*) and a knife, the type of which the Ripper may have used to murder and mutilate his victims with (*bottom*).

Prince Albert Victor, the Duke of Clarence, was among the suspects.

Suspects included James Maybrick.

A modern-day photograph of the Ten Bells in Fournier Street where some of the victims were said to have drunk.

poured scorn on Hay's assertion that Bury could have escaped. 'Supposing he was in an impecunious condition – and he had only 13s. – he could not have been in a position to have absconded.' The case for the Defence was that the wife committed suicide and the prisoner, angry with her for doing so, stabbed her and broke her legs and packed her away in a box.

Lord Young asked the jury not to attach much importance to the scream. It might have been a dream or it might have come from another home, so the evidence was not of first-class importance. Lord Young added that cases of suicide by strangulation were very rare but then said he had to dissent from the view taken by Mr McKechnie of Dr Lennox's evidence. Dr Lennox's evidence, said Lord Young, had been given properly and with propriety. Lord Young finished by saying that if the jury thought this woman did not commit suicide, then the only alternative verdict was that the prisoner had cruelly done her to death.

Lord Young had spoken from 8.50 p.m. till 10.05 p.m. The jury retired to consider its verdict and returned after 25 minutes.

McKechnie's mistake had been to lampoon Dr Lennox. This forced Lord Young to dissociate himself from McKechnie's remarks and meant that Lord Young appeared to give weight to Dr Lennox's testimony. If McKechnie had not delivered a personal attack on Dr Lennox, then Lord Young would not have defended the doctor. But when Lord Young told the jury to discount the scream, it meant the only evidence that a murder had been committed came from the medical evidence. But Lord Young had said that Dr Lennox's evidence that there was no sign of bruising on the body and that it was possible for Ellen Bury to have strangled herself was given 'properly and with propriety'.

When the verdict came, it caused quite a stir. The Clerk of the Court read out the names of the jury and, everyone having answered, he said, 'Gentlemen, what is your verdict?'

John Ramsay, Foreman of the Jury, answered, 'The jury unanimously find the prisoner guilty as libelled [charged] but strongly recommend him to the mercy of the court.'

Lord Young intervened. 'On what grounds do you recommend him to mercy?'

The Foreman gave no answer, as if he could not think of a reason. Lord Young asked the question again. This time another juryman, a local jeweller called Alexander Macpherson, answered, 'Partly on the ground of the conflicting medical evidence.'

A titter of laughter ran around the court. In an astonished tone, Lord Young said, 'The verdict, in fact, is equal to this – we find the prisoner guilty as libelled but being doubtful about the medical evidence recommend him to mercy. It was just the sort of verdict that nobody expects to hear in a Scotch court or anywhere out of Ireland.' Lord Young then made it clear that he was not going to accept the verdict. 'There is no ground for your recommendation to mercy there. I am afraid I must ask you to reconsider your verdict, as at present it leaves a doubt as to whether you are satisfied of the prisoner's guilt. You must retire again.'

The scene in the court was described in the *Dundee Advertiser* as follows:

> The Court-Room was very crowded and half at least of the audience was feminine. It cannot be said of the jury that its appearance suggested high intelligence, nor can it be said that one of the verdicts which in the end it returned suggested that the jury was better than its appearance . . .
> It was worthy of note that not a member of the jury asked a single question at any time during the trial.

The jury retired again but this time there was a buzz of excitement around the court. William Bury lost his composure and looked disturbed: 'his hands moved nervously', reported the *Dundee Advertiser*. Many in the court wondered if he would escape the guilty verdict that had been so widely anticipated. McKechnie's blunder had put the guilty verdict in jeopardy.

The jury was absent for only five minutes and then returned. After taking their places in the jury box, Lord Young addressed them, 'What is your verdict, gentlemen?'

This time the foreman said, 'We find the prisoner guilty as libelled.'

Lord Young turned to the prisoner. 'William Henry Bury,' he said, 'the sentence which must follow on the verdict returned against you is appointed by law.' His lordship paused to put on the black cloth before he continued:

> I do therefore, in the language and in the form prescribed for

me by law and custom, order and adjudge that you be carried from here to the Prison of Dundee, and therein detained until 24 April next, and upon that day, between the hours of eight and ten o'clock forenoon, within the walls of the said Prison of Dundee, by the hands of the common executioner, be hanged by the neck from a gibbet till you be dead, and thereafter to be buried within the walls of the prison; and I order that your movable goods and gear be escheated to Her Majesty the Queen, and this I pronounce for your doom; and may God have mercy on your soul.

It was 11 p.m. The trial had lasted only 13 hours.

11

THE SENTENCE OF DEATH

THERE HAD NOT BEEN A HANGING IN DUNDEE FOR OVER 40 years. The scaffold had last been erected 16 years previously, in 1873, when Thomas Scobbie was convicted of murder, but Scobbie's sentence was later commuted to penal servitude for life. For the past 16 years, the scaffold had lain in storage (presumably in pieces) in the vaults underneath the Sheriff Courthouse. The City Architect was given the task of inspecting it to make sure it was still suitable for the purpose of hanging.

William Bury spent 25 days in prison awaiting execution. Much of this time he spent reading the Bible and he was visited every day by the Reverend Gough. There is no record of him receiving any other visitors. His cell was lit day and night with gas jets and also contained a fireplace. The furniture consisted of the usual bed and bedding, a table, a stool for the prisoner and a chair for the officer in charge. But with regular meals and a well-stoked fire, Bury was probably living better now than at any time in his life before.

It was the practice for police officers to keep a constant watch over condemned prisoners. They worked shifts through the nights and days, and even watched over him while he lay asleep in his bed.

Meanwhile, McKechnie's ill-judged address to the jury continued to have ramifications. D.J. Tweedie, Bury's solicitor, appealed to the Marquis of Lothian, who was then Secretary of State for Scotland. Tweedie's petition highlighted the fact that

Bury's mother was insane and put its emphasis on the two verdicts given by the jury, contending that – as no new facts were adduced after the jury retired to consider its verdict – the second verdict should have been 'Not Proven'.

At the same time, Reverend Gough – bizarrely – seemed to be writing to the Secretary of State for Scotland to ask him to reject the appeal as quickly as possible so that he could prepare William Bury to accept his fate.

> St Paul's Parsonage
> Dundee
> 15 April, 1889
>
> My Lord
> I hope that . . . you will pardon me if I ask you, as soon as you have considered the case of W.H. Bury, to let me know your decision with the least possible delay inasmuch as I find it impossible to make any progress in the preparation of the poor man for his end, while any hope remains of possible reprieve and thus the time mercifully given by law for such preparation is reduced to the narrow limits of the last few days . . . The date fixed for the execution is Wednesday week (24th) and I am most anxious to have a clear week if the man is really to die . . .
> Edward John Gough.

Gough's appeal appears to have had no effect because it was on 22 April, only three days before the execution, that Lord Lothian wrote to the Provost of the City of Dundee to inform him of his decision:

> Monteviot
> Ancrum
> 22 April, 1889
>
> Sir,
> With reference to the case of William Henry Bury, now lying under sentence of death in H.M. Prison, Dundee, I have to acquaint you that, after careful consideration, I am unable to discover any sufficient grounds to justify me in recommending Her Majesty to interfere in this case. The law will therefore take its course.

You will be good enough to acknowledge receipt of this intimation.

I am, Sir,

Your obedient servant,

Lothian.

Lord Lothian's refusal of Bury's appeal was dated 22 April but Bury's solicitor must have received prior warning, perhaps by telephone, because he was reported to have visited Bury on 21 April and informed him that the appeal had been rejected. The policemen on duty in Bury's cell noticed that he was fighting back the tears later that day and was unable to sleep for much of the night.

Next day, under the supervision of the Reverend Gough, William Bury wrote out a confession to the murder of his wife. This poses one obvious question: if he was Jack the Ripper, why did he not also confess to the murders he committed in Whitechapel? The game was up; he was going to the scaffold and there was no advantage in continuing to deny that he was Jack the Ripper. It could be argued, therefore, that the existence of a confession for the murder of his wife but not for any other crimes suggests that Bury was not, indeed, Jack the Ripper.

The confession read as follows:

H.M. Prison

Dundee

22 April, 1889

To the Reverend E.J. Gough

Having made to you as a clergyman a complete acknowledgement of the circumstances of the unhappy crime for which I am now here, I hereby give you authority to make public the following statement after my death – I admit that it was by my own hands that my wife Ellen Bury met with her death on 4th Feb in the house 113 Princes Street Dundee by Strangulation. But I solemnly state before God as a dying man that I had no intention of doing so before the deed was done. I have communicated to you my motive for the crime but as it concerns so closely the character of my wife, I do not wish you to make it known publicly.

And for this act of mine I ask the Pardon of Almighty

God trusting in His mercy to grant me that Pardon which he is ever willing to give to those who are deeply sorry and truly penitent for their sins.

I declare as a dying man that this is the absolute truth.

I remain your obediently,

William Henry Bury.

If Bury gave a truthful and honest confession, then there would be some force in the argument that he would also have confessed to any other crimes he might have committed. But the confession is deeply dishonest, as if Bury was so much in the habit of telling lies that he could not change his ways even on the eve of his execution.

Perhaps the most telling phrase in the confession is the one in which Bury says he has told the Reverend Gough his motive for the murder, 'but as it concerns so closely the character of my wife I do not wish you to make it known publicly'. In other words, Bury is saying that his wife drove him to the act of murder. It is her fault because of her character or her behaviour and Bury, being the gentleman he is, wishes to protect her reputation by refraining from publicly disclosing his wife's repellent character but, of course, the Reverend Gough knows and understands the situation.

This is ludicrous. The confession is not a confession at all. Bury is presenting himself as the innocent party and putting the blame for the murder on to his wife. This is not the confession of a man who genuinely wants to make his peace with God – he is still trying to fool people. In a subtler and more devious way, he is persisting with the plea of innocence he made at the trial. The tone of the confession is such that he could not have added confessions to other crimes because he is not admitting guilt for anything.

It is worth noting at this point his statement on the morning of his execution: 'This is my last morning on earth. I freely forgive all who had given false evidence against me at my trial, as I hope God will forgive me.'

Who gave false evidence against him? He had, by this time, confessed to the murder of his wife, so how could he argue that anyone at the trial had given false evidence? What motive could he have had for making such a statement when his appeal had failed and no amount of protestations would now save his neck?

The only conclusion one can draw is that Bury was incapable of telling the truth and incapable of taking responsibility for his actions. He was acting out a performance in which he was going to his death still trying to deceive all those around him.

It would not have been consistent for Bury to have admitted to other crimes whilst also trying to present an image of himself as an innocent party, driven to this murder by the character of his wife. Therefore, the confession proves nothing: it is another attempt to deceive from a man who was a congenital liar.

On Thursday, 24 April, Bury awoke at 5 a.m. and lay in bed for 15 or 20 minutes before getting up. This morning, he was allowed to dress not in his usual prison garb but in the tweed suit he had worn at his trial. Between 6 and 7 a.m., Bury was given a breakfast of tea, bread and butter and poached eggs. At about 7.15 a.m., the Reverend Gough entered his cell. The clergyman was to remain with him till the end.

The hangman, whose name was James Berry, entered Bury's cell at 7.55 a.m. and bound his hands. Then, followed by the Reverend Gough, James Berry led his prisoner out of the cell and into the corridor, where William Geddes, the Prison Governor, was waiting with some of the City Magistrates. Some seats and a desk had been put in the corridor that morning for the officials' use.

When William Bury was taken in front of the magistrates, the Prison Governor (William Geddes) handed them the warrant and said, 'Gentlemen, this man is William Henry Bury and this warrant is applicable to him.' The magistrates signed the death warrant and then joined the procession to the scaffold. A slight commotion was caused when the executioner abruptly halted the procession and removed Bury's collar and tie: he was baring the condemned man's neck for the noose. He slipped the white hood over Bury's head and the prisoner now had to be helped along the last ten yards to the scaffold. The hood was put over his head early to prevent him breaking down when he first set eyes on the scaffold.

Bury was reported to be 5 ft 3½ in. tall and to weigh 9 st. 10 lb. A drop of 6½ ft was calculated as necessary by the hangman. After a few words from the Reverend Gough, Bury's legs were strapped together and the noose was placed over his head. At eight o'clock precisely, the hangman pulled back the lever, the trapdoors opened and William Bury disappeared from view. A sudden jerk of the rope a moment afterwards was followed by a dull thud. According to the *Dundee Courier* the next day, 'The rope never gave a quiver, indicating that death was instantaneous.' Two hours after the execution, James Berry, public hangman, boarded a southbound train at Tay Bridge Station and left Dundee. The body of William Bury was interred within the walls of Dundee Prison.

The *Courier* felt moved to publish the following article:

THE EXECUTION OF BURY

It is to be presumed that justice was satisfied by the dread tragedy enacted yesterday morning within the walls of Dundee Prison. There are still to be found persons who profess that when one murder has taken place a second should follow. Yesterday's proceedings amounted to nothing less than cold-blooded murder. In every detail the cruelty of the whole business was positively savage. Beginning with the scene at which the miserable criminal was told the day and hour his life would be taken from him, continuing through the intervening weeks, during which he was carefully watched lest he should voluntarily shorten the agony of thought, and terminating in the callous brutality witnessed by officialdom and magisterial pomp, the drama was of the most revolting description. It possessed not one feature entitling it to the sacred name of justice. Yet those who are opposed to capital punishment are loftily told they are mere sentimentalists, who indulge in sickly notions that, if acted upon, would plunge the whole empire into anarchy and disorder. According to the superior beings who make that statement, it is necessary to perpetuate judicial butcheries such as that of yesterday in order that the criminal classes may be properly kept in check . . . To the 'sentimentalists', on the other hand, it is not pleasant to be assured that it is incumbent upon men to slay one or two of their fellow-creatures occasionally for the purpose of keeping humanity human.

Part Two

LONDON, 1888

12

POLLY NICHOLS

SEVEN WOMEN WERE MURDERED IN THE EAST END OF LONDON in 1888. Of these only five are generally regarded as being victims of Jack the Ripper, while only two murders are significant in terms of the identification of William Bury as a possible suspect: those of Annie Chapman and Mary Jane Kelly. Interestingly, perhaps, a man fitting Bury's description was seen with the fifth victim (Mary Jane Kelly) on the day of her murder. Sadly, the description was not a good one and would have fitted a lot of other men who inhabited London at that time. But we will look at this in more detail when we come to the murder of Mary Jane Kelly.

The first woman to be murdered in Whitechapel in 1888 was Emma Smith. She was walking home between 4 a.m. and 5 a.m. on 3 April when she was assaulted and robbed by three men. She died of her injuries two days later. She is not regarded as a victim of Jack the Ripper.

The second woman to be murdered was Martha Tabram (or Turner); her body was found on the first-floor landing of George Yard Buildings at 4.45 a.m. on Tuesday, 7 August. Her clothes had been disarranged as if she had been struggling with someone and she had been stabbed 39 times. She had been lying there at least since 3.30 a.m. when a tired workman, on his way home to bed, had passed her as he climbed the stairs. He paid no attention because he was used to seeing homeless people sleeping on the landing.

Tabram's murder carries some of the hallmarks of a Ripper

murder. She was a prostitute and there seems to have been no motive for the killing. The cause of death may have been strangulation, because none of the tenants of George Yard Buildings heard noises of a struggle, such as a woman screaming. It is possible that death was caused by strangulation and that the wounds in the body were inflicted afterwards, which seems to be the way that the Ripper worked.

However, Tabram was not mutilated in the way that the other Ripper victims were. She was stabbed repeatedly in the abdomen, indicating a frenzy of excitement on the part of the killer. Although this is similar to the way in which the Ripper worked, it is not identical. Jack the Ripper did stab his victims but he would also make longer cuts, as if he were a surgeon dissecting a body. He seemed to work in a more cool-headed, cold-blooded way, taking time to slice open his victims and look inside.

Whoever killed Tabram had worked himself up into such a frenzy of excitement that he delivered 39 stabs into her abdomen after he strangled her to death. In the absence of any known motive, it is hard to avoid coming to the conclusion that this was a sexual murder. But the other victims do not seem to have been killed by a man who had worked himself up into a frenzy of excitement. Against this, it has to be said that Tabram was killed silently and efficiently – like the other Ripper victims. And sadistic pleasure seems to have been the motive for the mutilations inflicted on Tabram and the others.

Most of the victims of Jack the Ripper were, like Tabram, found in the street. Prostitutes did not merely solicit in the streets; they also had to perform the sex act there. To minimise the risk of being caught by a policeman on the beat, a dark and shadowy corner would be sought. The woman would probably bend forward and lift her skirts; the man would enter from the rear. Alternatively, the woman may have stood facing the man to allow him to enter from the front. In both cases, the sex act was performed standing up.

Contraception would probably have been practised in one of three ways. The first would be *coitus interruptus*, in which the penis is withdrawn from the vagina prior to ejaculation. Equally possible is the fact that the woman may have held the penis between her thighs until the man ejaculated. The third possibility is that sausage skins may have been used as a sheath.

However, the main risk that the prostitutes ran was of being caught by a policeman. London was patrolled by policemen walking in circular beats all around the city. A policeman would walk down one street, then another and another till he eventually found himself back in the street he had started in. Then he would do the whole manoeuvre again, and again . . . for hour after hour until he had finished his shift. And the same street might be crossed by two or more policemen walking different beats. A prostitute, or a murderer, working the open streets was constantly at risk of being caught.

In fact, a policeman on the beat saw a soldier loitering at the north end of George Yard at about 2 a.m. on the night of Tabram's murder. She had been seen by another prostitute taking a soldier to George Yard and it was believed that at least one of her wounds was inflicted with a bayonet. For this reason, it is not known if or if not she was a Ripper victim. It is clearly possible that the soldier had killed her.

However, it is also possible that the first floor of George Yard Buildings was a quiet spot in which Tabram did a lot of her business. Therefore, she may have gone on to the streets looking for more custom after she left the soldier; she may then have met another man and taken him to George Yard.

If William Bury could be proven to have been in Wolverhampton on 7 August 1888, then he must be discounted as a possible murderer of Martha Tabram. Unfortunately, we do not know where Bury was on this date. We have already seen that Margaret Corney testified that William and Ellen Bury went to Wolverhampton for a fortnight in August. However, Corney may well have been mistaken because the Burys were definitely in London on 11 August, when they started their tenancy with William Smith. It is highly unlikely that the Burys were in Wolverhampton for a fortnight in August.

William Hay suggested to Corney that the Burys had stayed in Quickett Street after their marriage. Corney knew nothing about this, which may suggest that she did not know as much as she claimed about the Burys' movements during the summer of 1888.

It is possible that the Burys went to Wolverhampton in July and returned to London in August. Bearing in mind that Margaret Corney was interviewed six months afterwards, she may have become slightly confused about the dates. She gave no dates for the holiday in Wolverhampton but merely said that it was in August. How much Margaret Corney would know about the Burys' movements would depend on how much contact she had with her sister but, as we have seen, there does not seem to have been much contact between the sisters before October and it is surely significant that Margaret Corney does not seem to have attended her sister's wedding in April.

Although Margaret Corney is the only witness we have who gave evidence about William and Ellen Bury's movements between 23 April and 10 August 1888, she should *not* be regarded as an expert. All we can be certain of is that the Burys stayed with Elizabeth Haynes for three weeks after their marriage on 2 April and that from 11 August they were in Spanby Road, Bow.

So where was William Bury living on 7 August when Tabram was killed? There are four possibilities: in Wolverhampton itself, or in Quickett Street, Blackthorn Street or Sunbury Street in London. There may even be a fifth possibility. The date of 11 August is the date of the start of their tenancy with William Smith but it cannot be assumed that they were travelling back from Wolverhampton on 10 August. If they returned to London from Wolverhampton in the first week of August, they may have taken temporary accommodation in, for example, a common lodging house while looking for something more permanent.

The five murders generally regarded as the work of Jack the Ripper began on Friday, 31 August. The first body was found shortly before four o'clock in the morning when Charles Cross spotted something like a tarpaulin lying in a gateway as he walked down Bucks Row. Bucks Row was a dark and quiet street, lit only by the feeble glow from one solitary gas lamp at the far end. But as Cross drew closer, he realised that he was looking at the body of a woman.

Cross went over to the body and stared at it. When another man came walking along the street, he stepped on to the roadway to pass Cross but Cross stepped towards him, touched him on the shoulder and said, 'Come and look at this woman here.'

The second man's name was Robert Paul. This was the moment when he first saw the woman, her clothes raised up almost to her stomach. Now the two men looked cautiously at the body, neither of them realising the woman had been murdered. Cross felt one of her hands, which was very cold. 'I believe she is dead,' he said. The men agreed the best thing they could do would be to fetch a policeman.

Paul decided to pull down the woman's clothing and, as he was doing so, put his hand over her heart and thought he felt a slight movement. 'I believe she is breathing,' he remarked. Neither of the men had seen any blood in the darkness. They both left the body and walked out of Bucks Row and into Bakers Row, where they spotted a police constable. They told him that there was a woman in Bucks Row either dead or drunk.

In the meantime, another policeman had already turned into Bucks Row. This was Police Constable John Neil, whose beat took him along Bucks Row in the direction of Brady Street. His beat was a very short one and could be covered in 12 minutes if he was walking quickly. This morning, though, he had taken a bit longer and about half an hour had elapsed since he last walked up Bucks Row.

Both Cross and Paul had left Bucks Row by the time PC Neil entered the street. He noticed the dim outline of a figure lying on the other side of the street and crossed the street to hold his lantern over the body. As soon as he did so, he noticed the blood oozing from a wound in the woman's throat.

The body was lying lengthways beside a closed gateway and the woman's left hand was touching the gate. She was lying on her back with her clothes disarranged. Her eyes were wide open, which must have been disconcerting for PC Neil, as he felt her arm and found that the upper part was still warm.

PC Neil then heard PC John Thain passing the top of Bucks Row. He attracted his attention by flashing his lantern and shouted, 'Run at once for Dr Llewellyn!' Spotting another constable in Bakers Row (presumably PC Jonas Mizen who had spoken to Charles Cross), Neil called to him and told him to go to Bethnal Green Police Station to fetch an ambulance.

Dr Llewellyn's surgery was about 300 yards away. The doctor dressed himself quickly and was at the scene of the crime within minutes. He made a hurried examination of the body and said, 'Move the woman to the mortuary: she is dead. I will make a further examination of her.' In his brief examination, Dr Llewellyn noticed that the hands and wrists of the woman were cold but that her lower extremities were warm. He guessed that the woman had been dead for about half an hour, which put the time of death at about 3.30 a.m.

Dr Llewellyn's estimate of the time of death was corroborated by PC Neil who had seen no sign of the dead woman when he last walked up Bucks Row at 3.15 a.m. PC Neil discovered the body almost exactly half an hour later at 3.45 a.m.

The killing had been carried out very efficiently. Patrick Mulshaw, a nightwatchman with Whitechapel District Board of Works, was on duty till 6 a.m. He stated that, between the hours of 3 a.m. and 4 a.m., he neither saw anyone about nor heard any cries or any other noise.

Mrs Emma Green was also sure that she would have heard a scream, had one been uttered. She was a light sleeper and was living in a cottage close to the spot where the body was found. She had gone to bed at 11 p.m. and slept until she heard a knock on her door at 4 a.m. It was only when she opened her window and looked out and saw a policeman that she realised there had been a murder.

As soon as the body had been taken away, Mrs Green's son went out into the street with a pail of water to wash the bloodstains off the pavement. Incredibly, a constable was in attendance as he did so! Later that morning, Inspector Helson went to the scene of the crime to look for clues and was surprised to find there were no bloodstains!

Once Dr Llewellyn had made his examination and pronounced the woman dead, the constables lifted up the body and put it in the ambulance. PC John Thain got a lot of blood on his hands and noticed that the woman's back was soaked with blood. The body was then taken to the mortuary in Old Montague Street, Whitechapel, where it was examined more thoroughly.

The mortuary, however, was to be the scene of yet another blunder. The body of the dead woman was left in the care of Robert Mann and James Hatfield, two pauper inmates of Whitechapel Workhouse. The police had apparently told them that a doctor was coming to examine the body but had not told them to leave the body untouched till then.

Thinking that they were doing the right thing, Mann and Hatfield began preparing the body for the doctor's post-mortem. They took off the ulster the dead woman had been wearing, followed by her jacket and her dress. She was also wearing two petticoats and they cut the straps of the garments and tore them down the front with their hands. A chemise suffered the same

114

treatment as the petticoats, Mann tearing it all the way down the front.

The only policeman to look at the body before the arrival of the doctor was Inspector Spratling. It was he who noticed that the victim had received deep wounds in her abdomen. This discovery immediately posed a problem for the police. The abdomen had been ripped open yet there had only been a small pool of blood in the street, at the spot where the woman's neck had been lying. This provoked theories that the woman had been murdered elsewhere and then dumped in Bucks Row. *The Times* delivered its view:

> If the woman was murdered on the spot where the body was found, it is almost impossible to believe she would not have aroused the neighbourhood by her screams, Bucks Row being a street tenanted all down one side by a respected class of people, superior to many of the surrounding streets, the other side having a blank wall bounding a warehouse. Dr Llewellyn has called the attention of the police to the smallness of the quantity of blood on the spot where he saw the body, and yet the gashes in the abdomen laid the body right open.

But the idea that the victim could have been killed elsewhere and then dumped in Bucks Row was simply not credible. There were a number of people (eight or more) awake in or near to Bucks Row at the time of the murder and none of them heard or saw a horse-drawn coach with wooden wheels rattling along the cobbled road to then stop, eject a body and drive on.

So how could the victim have been murdered in Bucks Row without anyone hearing her screams? A police constable had been on duty at the Great Eastern Railway Yard, only 50 yards from the spot where the body was found, and had heard nothing. Mrs Purkiss, who lived in Bucks Row, had also heard nothing despite the fact that she had been pacing the floor of her room at the time of the murder.

It seems likely that the murderer struck the woman a blow on the head to stun her (the victim had bruises on her face) and then strangled her. This would explain why no one heard her screaming; she was probably being strangled before she knew what was happening. It would also explain why there was so little blood on the street: if she was already dead when her throat was cut, then there would have been very little bloodstaining. Only if the heart is beating will blood spurt out like a fountain.

In his book *The Complete Jack the Ripper*, Donald Rumbelow argues convincingly that Jack the Ripper strangled his victims before cutting their throats and mutilating them. Rumbelow states that strangulation followed by mutilation would have resulted in much of the blood being absorbed by the victim's clothes, which seems to be precisely what happened. Rather than spurting out quickly and with a lot of force, the blood would have oozed out slowly. Bearing in mind that PC Thain got a lot of blood on his hands when he touched the woman's back, it is safe to say that the strangulation theory is consistent with the known facts.

The inquest, presided over by Coroner Wynne Baxter, picked its way through the meagre evidence. Given that there were three night watchmen and four policemen in the area, Coroner Baxter found it difficult to believe that the killer had been able to get away without being seen:

> It seemed astonishing, at first thought, that the culprit should escape detection, for there must surely have been marks of blood about his person. If, however, blood was principally on his hands, the presence of so many slaughterhouses in the neighbourhood would make the frequenters of that spot familiar with blood-stained clothes and hands, and his appearance might in that way have failed to attract attention while he passed from Bucks Row in the twilight into Whitechapel Road and was lost sight of in the morning's market traffic.

The dead woman's name was Mary Ann Nichols, although she was more commonly known as Polly Nichols. She was 42 years old and had been married to William Nichols, a printer's machinist, for 22 years. For the past eight years, she had lived apart from her husband. He had left her for another woman, allegedly because of Polly's persistent drinking. It is not disputed that Polly Nichols had a drink problem but there is a difference between an excuse and a reason: her drinking may have been the excuse her husband used to justify leaving her for another woman. The couple seem to have separated and got back together a number of times before complete marital breakdown took place.

Polly Nichols had five children by her husband William. By 1888, one of these children was being looked after by their maternal grandfather. The others must have been living with their father because they most certainly were not being looked after by Polly. At the time of her death, she had not seen her husband for three years nor her father for two. She had been in and out of workhouses for years but in April 1888, got a lucky break when she was offered a job as a domestic servant by a lady in Wandsworth. Instead of turning over a new leaf, however, Polly stole £3 and absconded.

For the last three weeks of her life, she lived as a lodger in a common lodging house at 18 Thrawl Street, Spitalfields. She shared a room there with three other women. Each paid 4d. a night and slept in separate beds.

When Polly turned up at the lodging house late on Thursday, 30 August, she was refused admission by the deputy because she did not have enough money to pay for her bed. She was described as being the worse for drink but not drunk and went away laughing, saying, 'I'll soon get my doss money; see what a jolly bonnet I've got now.' She was wearing a bonnet that she had not been seen with before.

She was last seen alive at 2.30 a.m. on Friday morning, standing in Whitechapel Road on the corner of Osborn Street. She had not yet fully sobered up and was staggering against a wall when a woman who knew her passed by. The woman, whose name was Mrs Holland, stopped and spoke to her. When Polly told her that she had no money, Mrs Holland offered to try to get her into her own lodging house. Polly, however, refused. She said that she had had her lodgings money three times that day but had spent it and was now going to try to get some more.

Sometime during the next hour she met her killer.

13

ANNIE CHAPMAN

ALBERT CADOSCH LIVED AT 27 HANBURY STREET, SPITALFIELDS. On Saturday, 8 September, he rose shortly before 5.30 a.m. and went into the yard at the back of the house (presumably to go to the toilet). Returning across the yard to his house, he heard a voice say, 'No!' in the backyard next door. He went into his house and then back out into the yard about three or four minutes later. This time, he heard something fall against the tall wooden fence which separated his backyard from that of No. 29.

Cadosch took no notice but walked out of the yard and went on his way to work. When he passed Spitalfields Church, he noticed that it was now 5.32 a.m. Much later, he would find out that, if he had dallied in the yard another five minutes, he would have seen Jack the Ripper come hurtling over the fence.

At 5.45 a.m., John Davis rose and went down to the yard. He had a room at 29 Hanbury Street which he shared with his wife and three sons. He only rarely enjoyed an undisturbed night's sleep because his sons would come home at different times.

The front of the house faced Hanbury Street but a passage ran from the front door through to the backyard. Both the front door and the one leading into the yard were never locked and both were often left open all night long. Davis had never known the doors to be locked, which meant that anyone who knew the area could open them and walk through to the yard. This morning, the back door was shut but the front door was wide open. Davis pushed open the back door and got the fright of his life.

He turned and rushed out into the street, where he saw James

Kent and James Green. They were packing-case makers who had arrived a little too early to start work and were waiting for their workmates to arrive. Davis shouted, 'Men, come here!' Green and Kent went over but it was Kent who went through the passageway first. He came to a sudden stop when he reached the back door.

Stone steps led down to the yard, which was about four feet below the level of the passage. The body of a dead woman was lying along the side of the fence with her head almost touching the steps. She was lying on her back with her clothes disarranged and her head almost severed from her body. Once again, the abdomen had been slashed open. The apron she was wearing appeared to have been thrown over her, perhaps cast down by the murderer after wiping his hands.

Blood was smeared over the woman's face and hands, as if she had been struggling. Her hands were raised and bent, with the palms towards the upper part of her body, suggesting that she had been fighting to protect her throat and trying to resist an attempt to strangle her. There were marks of blood about her legs but James Kent did not notice any on her clothes. By this time, he was so frightened that he had to drink some brandy to calm his nerves. He then went to a shop for a piece of canvas to throw over the body but by the time he returned the police had arrived and a mob had already assembled outside the front door.

Hanbury Street ran from Commercial Street to Bakers Row, the end of which was near Bucks Row. People began to talk about the proximity of the two crimes. The newspapers were about to start referring to the 'Whitechapel murders'.

Dr Bagster Phillips arrived on the scene at 6.30 a.m. The first thing he noticed was that there were spots of blood around the body and on the wall. The largest spot of blood found in the yard was about the size of an old sixpenny piece. He then gave the body a brief examination, noticing that one or more rings had been torn from the dead woman's left hand. When the doctor was finished, the body was taken away to the mortuary in Old Montague Street in the same shell or coffin in which the body of Polly Nichols had been carried off.

Dr Phillips had also found a piece of coarse muslin and a pocket comb in a paper case lying at the woman's feet. It looked to him as if they had been placed there deliberately, although he could not think why the woman's assailant should want to do such a thing.

It is worth mentioning at this point that the legend grew up, years later, that coins and rings had been neatly laid at the feet of the dead woman by the killer. But Richard Whittington-Egan, in *A Casebook on Jack the Ripper*, questioned the legend by stating that there was no mention of the discovery of any such articles in the original evidence of either Dr Bagster Phillips or Inspector Joseph Chandler.

Once the body had been removed, the police carefully searched the yard and found the torn portion of an envelope which was stained with blood. It had the crest of a Sussex Regiment on it and the date 'London, August 20' but the name and address was missing with the sole exception of the letter 'M'. On the other side were the letters 'Sp'. Two pills were also found in the yard and they were picked up by the police.

William Stevens of 35 Dorset Street, who knew the dead woman, later stated that she had picked up the piece of envelope from the fireplace at 35 Dorset Street. Even if Stevens was mistaken, the envelope is useless as evidence. The letter 'M' was probably the first letter of the words 'Mr', 'Mrs' or 'Miss', and 'Sp' was likely to have been the first letters of the word 'Spitalfields' – indicating that a letter may have been sent to someone living in Spitalfields by someone in the Sussex Regiment.

The pills were equally useless as evidence because they could have been dropped by any one of the seventeen people living at 29 Hanbury Street. It was statistically unlikely that the pills had been dropped by the killer but, even if they had, there were no conclusions that could be drawn. Most certainly, the existence of two pills did not prove that the killer was a doctor; all they proved was that he might have had two pills in his possession.

Infuriatingly, lessons had not been learned from the Polly Nichols post-mortem and more evidence was about to be destroyed. The body was left by police in the care of Mary Elizabeth Simonds and Frances Wright. The two women were nurses at Whitechapel Infirmary and they stripped and washed the body before a doctor arrived to conduct the post-mortem.

Once he had completed the post-mortem, Dr Phillips strongly suggested that the cause of death was strangulation when he said that the dead woman's breathing had been interfered with before death. The deceased had a swollen and protruding tongue and swollen face, which were signs of suffocation. The throat had been severed afterwards, with jagged incisions reaching right around the neck.

The victim also had a bruise over the right temple, a bruise on an eyelid and two bruises on the chest. The abdomen had been cut open and the intestines placed on the shoulder of the deceased. Phillips reckoned that the weapon used was a very sharp knife with a thin, narrow blade at least six to eight inches long and probably longer.

This time, there was less controversy about whether or not the murder was committed where the body was found. The supposition that the murder might have been committed elsewhere was again mooted because so little blood was found beside the body. This, however, was explained by the amount of blood the clothes would absorb and by Dr Phillips's indications that suffocation or strangulation may have been the cause of death with the mutilations to the throat and abdomen being inflicted on an already dead body. Furthermore, the police had not found a trace of blood on the walls or floor of the passage leading from Hanbury Street to the backyard. It seemed highly unlikely, if not impossible, that a body could have been dragged along the passageway without leaving a trail of blood and without disturbing Mrs Hardyman and her son, past whose bedroom door the murderer had to go.

There was also some evidence indicating that the murderer had been disturbed either by a noise coming from Hanbury Street or by a person at the front door of No. 29. If there had been no one about, the natural thing for the killer to have done would have been to calmly make his exit along the passageway and out into Hanbury Street hoping that no one would look at him too closely if he did not act suspiciously. Instead, he seems to have panicked and made his escape through the backyards of Nos. 27 and 25. Considering that Albert Cadosch had been in the backyard of No. 27 only moments earlier, this was a very risky thing to have done.

It was in the backyard of No. 25 that a little girl noticed peculiar marks on the wall and on the ground. She told Detective Inspector Chandler when he visited the property in order to make a plan of the backyard premises of all three houses for the use of the coroner at the inquest. Chandler examined the whole of the yard and found a bloody trail which ran for five or six feet in the direction of the back door of the house.

There was a mark like a smear on the wall of No. 25 that was also thought to have been made by the killer. Perhaps his bloodstained coat had brushed against the wall as he passed. Or, more likely, he may have tried to wipe some of the blood off his coat by wiping it on the wall before he walked out into Hanbury Street.

Abutting the end of the yard were Bailey's packing-case works. In an out-of-the-way corner of Bailey's yard, the police found some crumpled paper which was heavily stained with blood. It seems that the murderer had found the paper in the yard of No. 25 and had thrown it over the wall into Bailey's premises after wiping his hands on it.

The dead body discovered by John Davis was identified as that of Annie Chapman. She was 47 years old and had been separated from her husband for several years. Her husband's name was John Chapman and he was a coachman at Windsor. He had given her an allowance of ten shillings per week after they separated. Eighteen months later, the payments abruptly stopped and Chapman eventually learned that her husband was dead.

Now she had to earn a living as best she could. She moved in with a man who made iron sieves, which earned her the nickname Annie 'Siffey' or 'Sievey'. Sometime later, the sievemaker left her and she was forced to earn a living on the streets. The money she got from prostitution no doubt paid for a bed in the common lodging houses of Whitechapel and Spitalfields. She was also able to earn money by doing crochet work or by selling flowers and it was no secret what this money was spent on: Chapman was frequently seen the worse for drink.

Chapman's murder drew attention to the common lodging houses or doss houses that infested Whitechapel and Spitalfields. On 11 September 1888, *The Times* put forward its own theory about the apparent ability of the murderer to escape unseen from the scenes of the crimes:

> A visit to Dorset Street, which runs parallel with Spitalfields Market from Commercial Street, reveals the fact that nearly every house in the street is a common lodging house, in which the wretched human beings are,

at certain seasons of the year, crammed from cellar to roof. The streets leading into Dorset Street, where the woman was last seen alive, are also occupied by lodging houses. In Hanbury Street, Deal Street, Great Garden Street and several smaller thoroughfares houses of the same sort are located, and are frequented by the poorest class of the 'casual' community . . . The woman Chapman was known in appearance to the policemen on the night beats in the neighbourhood but none of those who were on duty between 12 and 6 on Saturday morning recollect having seen her. It was ascertained that several men left their lodgings after midnight with the expressed intention of returning who have not returned. Some men went to their lodgings after 3 o'clock, and left again before 6 in the morning, which is not an infrequent occurrence in these houses. None of the deputies or watchmen at the houses have any memory of any person stained with blood entering their premises but at that hour of the morning little or no notice is taken of persons inquiring for beds. They are simply shown up dark stairways with a bad light to their rooms. When they leave early, they are seldom noticed in their egress. It is then considered quite probable that the murderer may have found a refuge for a few hours in any one of those places, and even washed away the signs of his guilt. The men in these houses use a common washing-place, and the water once used is thrown down the sink by the lodger using it. All this might happen in a common lodging house in the early morning without the bloodstained murderer being noticed particularly. The conviction is growing, even, that taking for granted that one man committed all the recent murders of women in the Whitechapel district, he might in this fashion, by changing his common lodging house, evade detection for a considerable time.

Shortly before her murder, Annie Chapman had a fight with a woman called Eliza Cooper. Some of the bruises on the body examined by Dr Phillips were inflicted not by the Ripper but by Eliza Cooper. However, the two women had told completely contrasting tales as to the cause of the fight. According to Chapman, who before her death related the tale to her friends, she had gone to a public house with a man called Ted Stanley on Saturday, 1 September. She met Eliza Cooper, who was with a man called 'Harry the Hawker' in the public house. Chapman, who was drunk, put down a florin (two shillings) and Cooper slyly picked it up and replaced it with a penny. Chapman, though, was sober enough to notice. The women argued and, later that day, Cooper struck Chapman and caused bruising on her temple and chest.

Eliza Cooper's story was very different. She said that she, along with Chapman and many others, lived at a common lodging house at 35 Dorset Street. In Cooper's version, the fight with Chapman took place not on the Saturday but on the Tuesday before her murder. However, it stemmed from an incident that had taken place on Saturday when Chapman had come into the lodging house and asked for a piece of soap. She was told to ask Liza, which she did. Cooper then gave her a piece of soap and saw her hand it to Ted Stanley, who went away to have a wash. Chapman went out without returning the soap and when she came back Cooper asked her for it. Chapman did not return it this time, either, saying, 'I will see you by and by.'

The following Tuesday, Cooper met Chapman in the kitchen and again asked her to return the soap. Chapman threw a halfpenny piece on the table and said, 'Go and get a halfpennyworth of soap.' Cooper was unhappy about this and the women quarrelled. The quarrel broke out again later when they met in another public house. Chapman slapped Cooper's face and said, 'Think yourself lucky I did not do more.' Cooper retaliated by striking Chapman on the left eye and chest. One of the blows marked Chapman's face.

Cooper's more detailed account is the more convincing of the two but, in fact, it does not matter very much which of these two women was telling the truth: both accounts agree that it was Cooper – not Jack the Ripper – who gave Chapman a black eye and bruised her chest.

On Tuesday, 4 September, a woman called Amelia Farmer saw Chapman standing by the side of Spitalfields Church. Chapman complained to Farmer that she was feeling unwell and said she thought she would go into the casual ward for a day or two. She had had nothing to eat or drink that day, not even a cup of tea. Amelia Farmer gave her 2d., saying, 'Here is twopence to have a cup of tea, but don't have rum.'

Amelia Farmer next saw Chapman at 5 p.m. on Friday, 7 September. The women met in Dorset Street and, on this occasion, Chapman was sober. Farmer asked Chapman if she was going to Stratford but Chapman replied that she was too ill to do anything. Farmer left Chapman but saw her again a few minutes later. Chapman had not moved during the interval. She said to Farmer, 'I must pull myself together and go out and get some money, or I shall have no lodgings.' This was the last time Amelia Farmer saw her alive.

Chapman turned up at the common lodging house at 35 Dorset Street, Spitalfields, at 7 p.m. on Friday evening. Timothy Donovan was the deputy on duty and he asked where she had been all week because she had not been staying there. She told him that she had been in the infirmary. (This suggests that the two pills found in the yard where she was murdered may have belonged to her.) She then asked Donovan to let her go down to the kitchen, which he did.

She was still in the kitchen at 1.30 a.m. on Saturday morning. By this time, it was obvious that she had no intention of paying for a bed. Donovan went down to the kitchen and asked her for her lodging money. She said, 'I have not got it. I am weak and ill and have been in the infirmary.' Donovan told her that she knew the rules (i.e. that the rent of a bed had to be paid in advance), and that she would have to leave if she could not pay. She had been drinking but was able enough to walk erect, and Donovan said to her that she could find money for drink but not for a bed. Chapman replied that she had only been to the top of the street as far as Ringer's public house. But she left the lodging house, saying, 'I have not got any money now but don't let the bed; I will be back soon.'

Nothing is known of Chapman's movements over the next three hours. Between 4.40 and 4.45 a.m., John Richardson entered 29 Hanbury Street and went through to the backyard. He worked as a porter in Spitalfields Market and often gave No. 29 an inspection on his way to work because his mother lived there and the property had been broken into before.

The front door was closed when he arrived at the house. He lifted the latch and went through the passage to the yard door, which he pushed open. He did not go into the yard but stood on the stone steps and cut a piece of leather which was hurting his foot from one of his boots. Had Chapman's body been in the yard at this time, Richardson would obviously have noticed it. He then tied up the boot and went out, closing the front door behind him. It was getting light by this time.

The backyard of 29 Hanbury Street seems to have been a favourite spot for prostitutes. Rather than risking the embarrassment of being caught in the open street, the yard was a dark and quiet corner to which they could discreetly take their clients. John Richardson was accustomed to finding strangers either in the passage or in the yard during the night. He had found both men and women there and always chased them out.

At 5.30 a.m. on Saturday, 8 September, Elizabeth Long was passing down Hanbury Street and going to Spitalfields Market. She was certain of the time because a clock had newly struck. She was walking down the same side of the street as No. 29 when she saw a man standing on the pavement with Chapman and talking to her. They were standing close against the shutters of No. 29. The man had dark hair and wore a deerstalker hat. They were talking loudly.

Long heard the man say, 'Will you?' and Chapman replied, 'Yes.' They stood still as Long passed. Long thought the man had a foreign accent. She went on to her work without looking back.

Two minutes later, Albert Cadosch would hear something fall against the fence that separated the yard at 27 Hanbury Street from that of No. 29. (Once Chapman had been strangled, the killer would have let her body fall on to the ground before he began mutilating it.)

The man seen by Elizabeth Long must have been Jack the Ripper. There simply was not time for Chapman to have left her client and then found another and taken him into the yard and been murdered while Cadosch was passing on the other side of the fence.

Long cannot be blamed for not paying much attention to the couple as she passed on her way to work. Her description tells us nothing about the height and build of the killer. She says only that he wore a deerstalker hat and spoke with a foreign accent.

William Bury usually wore a hat but there is no evidence that he ever owned a deerstalker hat. When he was in Dundee, he appeared to have two hats – a felt hat and a satin hat.

But what did Long mean when she said the man had a foreign accent? The end of the nineteenth century was a period before mass communication such as radio. Only the rich could go on holiday, while those living in the East End were unlikely to have travelled. The only accents that Long would have been used to hearing would have been the accents of people she heard at work, in shops, in public houses and in the street. In those days, the poor would go to work and do their shopping within a short radius of their homes. Months, even years, might go by before a woman like Mrs Long had to leave her locality.

The critical question is this: had Elizabeth Long heard a Midlands accent before? The only way she would have known a Wolverhampton accent would be by meeting someone from the Wolverhampton area. Perhaps she knew what a Midlands accent sounded like and perhaps not: we will never know.

But it is possible that a Midlands accent may have sounded foreign to Long. She was not in the killer's company for any length of time but heard a snippet of conversation in an unfamiliar accent as she passed. She did not listen to the accent for any length of time and concluded that it was foreign. London, being a port, would have had its share of foreigners but we do not know what accents Long might have heard. We cannot assume that she had heard a Wolverhampton accent before and would recognise it. But there is one thing of which we can be sure: the man she heard did not speak with a local accent, which surely rules out all suspects who were Londoners.

By all accounts, the murder of Annie Chapman was an audacious crime committed in daylight as if the killer had no fear of being caught. But if the killer was seen before the murder, how had he managed to vanish into thin air after it? *The Times* eloquently posed this question in an article on 11 September:

> Intelligent observers who have visited the locality express the utmost astonishment that the murderer could have reached a hiding place after committing such a crime. He must have left the yard in Hanbury Street reeking with blood and . . . walked in almost broad daylight along streets comparatively well frequented, even at that early hour, without his startling appearance attracting the slightest attention.

But another article in the same edition of the newspaper offered a possible explanation:

The murderer must have known the neighbourhood, which is provided with no fewer than four police stations, and is well watched nightly, on account of the character of many of the inhabitants. On Saturday morning, between half past 4 o'clock and 6, several carts must have passed through Hanbury Street and at 5 o'clock, on the opening of the Spitalfields Market the end of which . . . was blocked with market vehicles, and the market attendants were busy regulating the traffic. In the midst of the bustle it is admitted that two persons might have passed through the hall of 29 Hanbury Street, and in consequence of the noise of passing vehicles, any slight altercation might have occurred without being overheard.

Luck also seemed to have been on the side of the killer. He had very nearly walked into a trap but had got away without anyone getting a proper glimpse of him. Coroner Wynne Baxter stated that 'the yard appeared to have been used by persons who had no legitimate business there'. Being a favourite haunt for many of the East End prostitutes, it would have been known to Chapman but probably not to her killer. She must have led him in there.

Speaking of 29 Hanbury Street, Coroner Baxter said:

It was built, like hundreds of others, for the Spitalfields weavers, and when hand looms were driven out by steam and power they were converted to dwellings for the poor. Its size was about such as a superior artisan would occupy in the country but its condition was such as would to a certainty leave it without a tenant. In that place 17 persons were living, from a woman and her son, sleeping in a cats' meat shop on the ground floor, to Davis and his wife and their three grown up sons, all sleeping together in the attic.

Baxter reckoned that the killer was almost certainly ignorant of 'the nest of living beings by whom he was surrounded, and of their occupations and habits. A carman named Thomson left the house as early as 3.50 a.m.; an hour later John Richardson paid the house a visit of inspection; shortly after 5.15 Cadosch, who lived in the next house, was in the adjoining yard twice.'

The day of Annie Chapman's murder saw yet more evidence being destroyed when a man was seen to be changing his clothes in the lavatory of the City News Rooms at Ludgate Circus. He left hurriedly, leaving behind his discarded clothes (a shirt, a pair of trousers and a pair of socks). The attendant threw the unwanted clothes in a dustbin and there they lay over the weekend until they were carted off in the city sewers cart the following Monday.

At about 7 a.m. on Saturday evening, 13 or 14 hours after the murder, another suspicious incident occurred in Grove Street, Deptford, Greater London. A man hurriedly entered a newsagent's shop and excitedly asked for a copy of the special edition of *The Star*, which contained an account of the latest Whitechapel murder. The newsagent told him that he had completely sold out and did not have one left. The man then asked for a special edition of the *Evening News* but such was the fever of excitement about the killings that it was also sold out.

'Then let me have a special anything,' the man said in frustration. The newsagent was at that moment reading the special edition of *The Standard* and he told the man that he could have that if he wished. The man snatched the paper from the surprised newsagent's hands, threw a penny on the counter and rushed outside to read it by the gaslight in the shop window. He seemed so agitated that the newsagent became suspicious and quietly slipped out of the shop to look for a policeman. There was a boy in the street and the newsagent told him to fetch a policeman as quickly as he could. The boy ran off down the street but when the newsagent went back into his shop, he was seen by the man. The man seemed to realise what had happened because he suddenly became alarmed, crushed up the newspaper and ran off in the direction of the Deptford and Southwark tramline, which would have taken him out of the neighbourhood in a few minutes.

The man was wearing an old felt hat pulled forward over his eyes and his coat collar was turned up, as if he was trying to hide his face. He was of stout build with a slight moustache and an unshaven appearance. He looked, in the words of the newsagent, 'as if a little soap would have done him good'.

The following day (Sunday, 9 September), a third suspicious incident occurred and was later reported in *The Times*:

A young woman named Lyons stated that at 3 o'clock yesterday afternoon she met a strange man in Flower and Dean Street. He asked her to come to the Queen's Head public house at half past 6 and drink with him. Having obtained from her a promise that she would do so he disappeared, and was at the house named at the appointed time. While they were conversing, Lyons noticed a large knife in the man's right-hand trousers pocket, and called another woman's attention to the fact. A moment later Lyons was startled by a remark which the stranger addressed to her. 'You are about the same style of woman as the one that's murdered,' he said. 'What do you know about her?' asked the woman, to which the man replied 'You are beginning to smell a rat. Foxes hunt geese but they don't always find 'em.' Having uttered these words the man hurriedly left. Lyons followed until near Spitalfields Church when, turning around at this spot and noticing that the woman was behind him, the stranger ran at a swifter pace into Church Street and was at once lost to view.

14

ELIZABETH STRIDE

TWO WOMEN WERE KILLED IN THE EARLY HOURS OF SUNDAY, 30 September, and a wave of panic swept through London. At 3 p.m. on Sunday, 12 hours after the murders, a meeting of nearly 1,000 people was organised in Victoria Park. Several speeches denounced the incompetence of the Home Secretary and Sir Charles Warren, Commissioner of the Metropolitan Police. A resolution was passed unanimously that it was high time both men resigned and made way for some others who would leave no stone unturned in their pursuit of the murderers 'instead of allowing them to run riot in a civilised city like London' (*The Times*, 1 October 1888).

Once again, it seemed incredible that the murderer could have escaped unseen – especially since an unsuspecting salesman called Louis Diemschutz must very nearly have caught the Ripper red-handed.

Diemschutz was described as a traveller in cheap jewellery. He left home at 11.30 a.m. on Saturday morning and travelled to Westow Hill, near Crystal Palace, where he spent the day doing business. It was very late at night when he went back home.

At exactly 1 a.m. on Sunday morning, Diemschutz drove his two-wheeled cart into the yard beside the International Working Men's Educational Club in Berner Street. Even though it was dark, Diemschutz could see that the big wooden gates were open and he steered the pony into the yard. Suddenly the animal shied. Diemschutz looked down at the ground and thought he could see something lying amongst the shadows. He poked about in the darkness with his whip but could not even guess what the object was.

Diemschutz jumped down from the cart and lit a match. Although the wind played havoc with the small flame, he got enough light to make out the body of a woman and immediately went into the Working Men's Club for help. This may have been the moment when the killer made his escape, sneaking out of the yard while Diemschutz entered the Working Men's Club by the side door.

This episode has become something of a mystery because Diemschutz was not carrying a lantern. That meant the yard was largely in shadow, except for the feeble light coming from the match. It seems likely that the killer was interrupted just as Diemschutz's horse came into the yard. That means that the killer must have hidden in the shadows while Diemschutz jumped down from the cart, lit his match and peered at the woman's body. This hypothesis is supported by the fact that there were gas lamps in Berner Street and that Diemschutz would surely have seen the killer if he had fled out of the yard as Diemschutz approached.

In the club, Diemschutz told his wife and several of the club members that there was a woman lying in the yard either dead or drunk. When he went back into the yard with a candle, he saw a trickle of blood running into the gutter, panicked and ran off through the streets shouting 'Police!' as loudly as he could.

The dead woman had been killed in a yard in Berner Street. The only entrance or exit to and from the yard was via the large wooden gates which had been open at the time of the murder. Walls on either side kept the yard in almost absolute darkness after sunset. On the right-hand side, the whole length of the yard was taken up by the Working Men's Club. There were also a number of cottages on the left-hand side and these were occupied mainly by tailors or cigarette makers. At the time of the murder, the only light in the yard was coming from the club because all the lights in the cottages were out. However, the lights from the club came from an upper storey where there was still some singing going on and fell only upon the cottages opposite, perhaps even serving to intensify the gloom inside the yard.

PC Henry Lamb was the first on the scene of the crime. By the time he arrived, news of the murder had already spread down the street and about 20 or 30 people were now in the yard where they crowded around the dead body. Lamb got the crowd to move back by saying, slightly threateningly, that if they came too close to the body and got some blood on their clothes they might get into trouble.

The wooden gates were quickly closed and no one was allowed in or out. More police arrived and they then searched the yard, the Working Men's Club and the cottages opposite in the faint hope that the killer might be hiding somewhere nearby. Once they had finished, the police searched and questioned each of the 28 people who had been in the yard when the gates were closed.

At this point, somebody realised that the toilets in the yard had not been searched; they were now carefully examined. The cottages were searched again and the occupants, who were in various states of undress, were questioned. A loft door was found to be locked and was broken down. But the bird had flown.

By this time, Dr Frederick Blackwell had also been and gone. He was one of the first to arrive in Berner Street, getting there at about 1.10 a.m. His attention was immediately drawn to the warmth of the body which, he reckoned, could only have been dead for 20 minutes at the longest. This is consistent with the theory that the killer was in the yard when Diemschutz arrived there at 1 a.m.

When Dr Blackwell made his examination, the dead woman was lying with her face turned to the wall and her feet nearly touching it. Her right hand, smeared on both sides with blood, was lying on her chest. The left hand was lying on the ground and tightly clasped a small packet of sweets. Many of these sweets had been scattered across the ground in the struggle. Her face was strangely placid, although her mouth was wide open. She was wearing a checkered silk scarf, which may have been used to strangle her because its bow had clearly been turned to the left and pulled tightly.

Unlike the other victims of Jack the Ripper, this woman's body had not been mutilated. Indeed, she might have been sleeping were it not for the long incision around her neck. The cut in her throat exactly corresponded with the lower edge of the scarf, which was slightly frayed, as if a knife had been drawn along it.

Even though it was the middle of the night, the news of the murder shot around the neighbourhood. Soon, the unusually quiet thoroughfare of Berner Street was thronging with crowds. Even with extra police posted all along the street, the crowds obstructed the passage of traffic from an early hour. A large crowd also followed the body to the mortuary, much to the annoyance of the police.

The dead woman's name was Elizabeth Stride. She was 45 years old and was of Swedish origin, having been born near Gothenburg. She had migrated to London more than 20 years before and had married a ship's carpenter called John Thomas Stride. Her husband had died about six years previously, after which she had become an irregular inhabitant of a common lodging house at 32 Flower and Dean Street.

For the preceding three years, she had flitted back and forth between the lodging house and the house of a waterside labourer called Michael Kidney, who lived at 38 Dorset Street. While Stride was living with Kidney, she often took the notion to leave him for several days at a time (presumably because they had quarrelled). On these occasions, she would go back to the lodging house at 32 Flower and Dean Street.

Michael Kidney last saw her alive on Tuesday, 25 September. He left her in Commercial Street when he was going to work. She was sober then and Kidney expected her to be at home when he returned; instead, he found that she had been in and gone out again.

Stride was seen in the Queen's Head public house in Commercial Street at 6.30 p.m. on Saturday. Between 7 p.m. and 8 p.m., she was in the kitchen of the lodging house at 32 Flower and Dean Street. She had slept there on the Thursday and Friday nights but it is not known where she was on the Tuesday night or all day Wednesday.

Stride had had some money because Elizabeth Tanner, a deputy at the common lodging house, had paid her 6d. on Saturday to clean the rooms. It was presumably this money which she spent in the Queen's Head. One of the last people to see her alive was William Marshall, a labourer living at 64 Berner Street. He was standing at his door, watching people coming and going up and down the street, from 11.30 p.m. till midnight. During this time, Marshall saw Stride talking to a man on the pavement about three doors away. The couple were talking quietly but Marshall could not see the man's face as there were no streetlamps nearby.

The man wore a small black cutaway coat, dark trousers and a round cap with a small peak like a sailor's cap. He was a stoutly built man about 5 ft 6 in. in height. He was decently dressed and Marshall thought he had the appearance of a clerk. He was also softly spoken and sounded very much like an educated man. Marshall also remembered that Stride was wearing a black skirt and a black jacket trimmed with fur.

The couple was standing between Marshall's door and the International Working Men's Club. When Marshall first saw them it was about 11.45 p.m. They then stood and talked for about ten minutes during which time the man kissed Stride and said, 'You would not say anything but your prayers.'

The couple sauntered down the street. The man's arms were around Stride's neck, it seemed affectionately. They were walking away from the Working Men's Club and went past Marshall but he still did not see the man's face, which was turned towards Stride.

The next person to see Stride was PC William Smith, who saw her about 40 minutes later. His beat took him along Berner Street and it was there that he saw a man with Stride at about 12.30 or 12.35 a.m. By this time, Stride had flowers in her jacket. The man that PC Smith saw with Stride was 5 ft 7 in. tall and wore a dark felt deerstalker hat and dark clothes including a dark cutaway coat and dark trousers. Smith thought the man was about 28 years of age. His description is close but not identical to the description given by Marshall except that the man Smith saw was carrying a newspaper parcel in his hand which was about eighteen inches long and six or eight inches wide.

The last person to see Elizabeth Stride alive was James Brown of 35 Fairclough Street. He was going from his own house to a chandler's shop at the corner of Berner Street, where he intended to buy something for his supper. It was 12.45 a.m. As he walked along Fairclough Street, he saw a man standing with Stride next to a wall and heard Stride say, 'No, not tonight, some other night.' That made Brown turn and look at them.

The man had his back to Brown and was standing with his arm up against the wall. The woman had her back to the wall and was facing the man. They were standing in the dark part of the street, making it difficult for Brown to see them. He thought the man was wearing a long coat which came down very nearly to his heels.

These three descriptions illustrate the problems faced by the police. Were these three descriptions of the same man or were they three different men? Could it even be descriptions of two men? Perhaps the first two descriptions are of the same man but the third description is of a different one.

Marshall said the man was 5 ft 6 in. tall. Smith, with his more experienced policeman's eye, said the man was 5 ft 7 in. tall. Both Marshall and Smith saw a man wearing a black cutaway coat and dark trousers but Marshall said he had a round peaked cap while Smith said he was wearing a deerstalker hat. The man that PC Smith saw was also carrying a newspaper parcel in his hand. The man that James Brown saw, on the other hand, was wearing a long coat that came down very nearly to his heels.

There are, in fact, two main questions here. Are these descriptions of the same man? And is any one of them a description of the killer?

The man seen by James Brown was seen with Stride about ten minutes before her murder. It is not impossible that Stride, in the space of ten minutes, could have left the man and met someone else who killed her. But it does seem logical to suggest that, at the very least, the man seen by James Brown is a strong suspect.

Coroner Baxter puzzled over this problem of the three witnesses and their different, but similar, descriptions:

> If they were correct in assuming that the man seen in the company of the deceased by the three was one and the same person it followed that he must have spent much time and trouble to induce her to place herself in his diabolical clutches. They last saw her alive at the corner of Fairclough St and Berner St, saying, 'Not tonight but some other night.' Within a quarter of an hour her lifeless body was found at a spot only a few yards from where she was last seen alive. It was late, and there were few people about but the place to which the two repaired could not have been selected on account of its being quiet or unfrequented. It had only the merit of darkness. It was the passageway leading into a court in which several families resided. Adjoining the passage and court there was a club of Socialists who, having finished their debate, were singing and making merry. The deceased and her companion must have seen the lights of the clubroom and

the kitchen, and of the printing office. They must have heard music and dancing, for the windows were open. There were persons in the yard but a short time previous to their arrival. At forty minutes past twelve, one of the members of the club, named Morris Eagle, passed the spot where the deceased drew her last breath, passing through the gateway to the back door which opened into the yard.

Coroner Baxter seemed to take the view that Marshall, Smith and Brown had all seen the same man. This is possible from the similar descriptions. But there could have been any number of suspicious-looking characters lurking around the East End that night. Consider the following statement made by Albert Backert of 13 Newnham Street, Whitechapel:

> On Saturday night, at about seven minutes to twelve, I entered the Three Nuns Hotel, Aldgate. While in there an elderly woman, very shabbily dressed, came in and asked me to buy some matches. I refused and she went out. A man who had been standing by me remarked that those persons were a nuisance to which I responded 'Yes.' He then asked me if I knew how old some of the women were who were in the habit of soliciting outside. I replied that I knew, or thought, that some of them who looked 25 were over 35. He then asked me whether I thought a woman would go with him down Northumberland Alley – a dark and lonely court in Fenchurch Street. I said I did not know, but supposed she would. He then went outside and spoke to the woman who was selling matches and gave her something. He returned, and I bid him goodnight at about ten minutes past twelve. I believe the woman was waiting for him. I do not think I could identify the woman, as I did not take particular notice of her; but I should know the man again. He was a dark man [dark-skinned], height about 5 ft 6 in. or 5 ft 7 in. He wore a black felt hat, a dark morning coat, a black tie and carried a black shiny bag.

This man sounds like the man seen by Messrs Marshall and Smith but cannot be because at that very moment he was talking to Albert Backert.

And another man, also carrying a black bag, was seen in

Berner Street very close to the time of the murder. Mrs Mortimer of 36 Berner Street lived only four doors from the scene of the murder and made the following statement which was quoted in *The Times*:

> I was standing at the door of my house nearly the whole time between half-past twelve and one o'clock on Sunday morning and did not notice anything unusual. I had just gone indoors when I heard a commotion outside and immediately ran out, thinking that there was a row at the Socialist club close by. I went to see what was the matter and was informed that another dreadful murder had been committed in the yard adjoining the club house and on going inside I saw the body of a woman lying huddled up just inside the gates with her throat cut from ear to ear. A man touched her face and said it was quite warm, so that the deed must have been done while I was standing at the door of my house. There was certainly no noise made, and I did not observe anyone enter the gates.
>
> It was just after one o'clock when I went out, and the only man I had seen pass through the street previously was a young man carrying a black, shiny bag who walked very fast down the street from the Commercial Road. He looked up at the club and then went round by the corner of the Board School.

Although this is an interesting statement, three things need to be borne in mind. First, Mrs Mortimer did not see anyone leave the Working Men's Club and therefore the man she saw walking down Commercial Road may not have fled from the club but may simply have been passing along the street. Second, it is not surprising that the man should look at the club if there was a commotion in the yard. And third, it was common for men to carry black leather bags.

It has been suggested that Elizabeth Stride was not a victim of Jack the Ripper because her abdomen had not been ripped open in the way that the others were. This theory means that the killer had intended to do no more than kill her by cutting her throat: it suggests that she may have known her killer and that there would have been a motive for the murder, although none has ever been suggested.

If Stride was not killed by Jack the Ripper, it means that the killer was not interrupted in his work and therefore suggests that the yard was empty when Diemschutz entered. But the time of death was so close to Diemschutz's arrival in Berner Street that this theory must be considered unlikely.

Dr Blackwell arrived on the scene at 1.10 a.m. He examined Stride's body and said she had been dead for 20 minutes *at the longest*. But Blackwell's guess allowed Stride to have been dead for a shorter time and it may also have taken Dr Blackwell a couple of minutes to make his diagnosis, meaning that the 20 minutes he estimated should not be counted from his arrival on the scene at 1.10 a.m. but from the time he finished his examination, which may have been something like 1.12 a.m. or 1.13 a.m.

If, for the sake of argument, Stride had been dead for 15 minutes and the time of Dr Blackwell's examination was 1.12 a.m. then that gives us a time of death of 12.57 a.m.

It should also be appreciated that the killer would have heard Diemschutz approach because he would have been certain to have heard the clip-clop of the horse's hooves on the cobbles in Berner Street. He may have had two or three minutes to find a hiding place in the yard before Diemschutz drove his cart through the gates at 1 a.m. This would also push the time of death back by a couple of minutes or so.

In fact, the time of death was so close to Diemschutz's arrival on the scene that the most logical conclusion to draw is that the killer was interrupted in his work; that he was in the yard when Diemschutz got down from his cart to look at the body; and that he made his escape when Diemschutz went into the Working Men's Club for help.

Mrs Mortimer had gone indoors shortly before 1 a.m. and then came back out when she heard a commotion. But the commotion did not arise until Diemschutz came back out with two or three members of the club. At the moment at which Diemschutz went into the club, Mrs Mortimer was inside her house. Therefore, there was time (perhaps two or three minutes) for the killer to make his escape unseen. But on this occasion he had not gone to work with his knife on the belly of his victim. He had, in fact, been deprived of his sport. He went off to look for another prostitute.

15

CATHERINE EDDOWES

MITRE SQUARE WAS A SMALL SQUARE ABOUT 15 MINUTES' WALK from Berner Street. It was made up mostly of commercial property, which meant the square was busy with the bustle of commercial traffic during the day and was then silent and empty at night.

The square was only 77 ft by 80 ft. Two sides of the square were taken up by the warehouses of Messrs Kearley and Tonge. Adjoining them were two old houses, one of which was unoccupied while the other was rented by a police constable. The rest of the square was made up of business premises.

George Morris was the nightwatchman who worked in the Kearley and Tonge warehouses. He had been on duty since 7 p.m. on Saturday evening but had heard or seen nothing unusual. It was now 1.45 a.m. on Sunday morning. Morris was doing some sweeping behind the front door, which was slightly ajar. He heard a knock on the door and saw it being pushed further open. Morris pulled open the door and found a policeman standing in the doorway. 'For God's sake,' said the policeman, 'come to my assistance.'

Morris's first thought was that the policeman must be ill. He asked him what was the matter. The PC was very agitated and replied, 'There is another woman cut to pieces.' Morris asked where the body was and was told, 'In the corner.'

Fortunately, perhaps, Morris had been a police constable before he became a nightwatchman and he now acted with great presence of mind. He immediately went over to the body and turned his lamp on it. A brief glance was enough to tell him that the woman was dead. He then left Mitre Square and ran up Mitre Street into Aldgate, looking for another policeman.

PC Watkins was the man who discovered the body. His beat took him through Mitre Square at 15-minute intervals. The murder had definitely been committed between Watkins's beats because he had looked into all the dark corners, passageways and warehouses when he passed through the square at 1.30 a.m. and had seen no one about.

When Watkins re-entered Mitre Square at 1.44 a.m., he turned his lantern on the darkest corner of the square and saw the lifeless body of a woman lying in a pool of blood. She was lying on her back with her feet pointing into the square. He did not touch the body but went across the street to the open door of Kearley and Tonge's warehouse door.

Again, the killer seemed to have come and gone as silently as a ghost. Sometime after 1.30 a.m. he had entered the square with his victim but George Morris had neither heard nor seen anyone – even though the door of the warehouse was slightly open.

There was even a policeman living in Mitre Square – PC Richard Pearse. From the window of his room, he had a clear view of the spot where the murder had been committed. He was asleep at the time of the murder and his sleep was not disturbed by any noises from the square until another policeman woke him at 2.20 a.m.

It seemed incredible that the killer had been able to do his work so silently. If his victim had managed to utter one scream, it would have been heard by George Morris and PC Watkins, and may also have woken up PC Pearse.

Dr George Sequeira was the first doctor to arrive on the scene. When he examined the body, it was lying on its back with its arms by its sides as if they had fallen there. There were no signs of a struggle. Both palms were turned upwards, which was reminiscent of the second victim, Annie Chapman. This time, the killer had had time to mutilate the body. There was a large gash across the face running from the nose on to the cheek, and part of the right ear had been cut off. As usual, the throat had been cut. The walls of the abdomen had also been cut open, from the breast downwards, and the intestines had been lifted out and dropped beside the victim's right shoulder.

This murder had been carried out with great daring. From 1.30 a.m., the killer had only 15 minutes in which to act before PC Watkins's beat brought him back into Mitre Square. Actually the killer had less than that time: he had to wait for PC Watkins to leave the square and also had to be gone by the time he returned.

As if that were not sufficient risk to run, the scene of the crime – Mitre Square – was a potential trap. It had three entrances: Mitre Street ran into the Square, as did passages from both Duke Street and St James's Place. The killer could easily have been surprised by pedestrians walking into the square from any one of these entrances. Moreover, the Square was so small that a policeman entering it at the right moment would very likely have been able to apprehend the murderer. 'The murder in the city was committed in circumstances which show that the assassin, if not suffering from insanity, appears to be free from any fear of interruption while at his dreadful work,' commented *The Times*.

For whatever reason, Jack the Ripper was now running high risks. Having committed a murder in a small square with three entrances where he could have been surprised at any time, he cut away a portion of the dead woman's apron and brazenly walked back in the direction of Berner Street. He must have been walking through the streets with the bloodstained apron in his hands while police whistles were blowing and policemen from all around were rushing towards Mitre Square.

Less than an hour had elapsed since the murder in Berner Street, yet the killer was confident enough to walk back in the direction of Berner Street for about one third of a mile before throwing the apron into a dark passage in Goulston Street. However, this action of his may not have been as mad as it sounds: he had to wipe the blood off his hands and off his knife and he could not do it in Mitre Square with PC Watkins due back at any moment. Hence, it made sense for the killer to wipe his hands on the move.

PC Alfred Long was on duty in Goulston Street, Whitechapel, early on Sunday morning. At about 2.55 a.m., he found the missing part of the apron. It was lying in a passage near the foot of a staircase that led to Nos. 118 and 119 Goulston Street (both were ordinary dwelling houses). Long could see that the apron was covered in blood and his first thought was that there was another body nearby. Above the apron was a cryptic message written on the wall in chalk. According to PC Long, the message read, 'The Jews are the men that will not be blamed for nothing.'

We do not know how much time the killer had had to get away before PC Watkins's beat took him back into Mitre Square – it may have been a few minutes or may only have been a few seconds – but with police whistles being sounded and policemen running about the streets, it seems unimaginable that the murderer would take the time to write a message on the wall of a house with the bloodstained apron of the last victim at his feet. It is very unlikely that the writing had anything to do with the murders. That, however, has not stopped a huge body of literature being built up about this writing, including portentous theories about secret conspiracies involving royalty or freemasons.

Detective Daniel Halse looked at the writing later that morning. He went to Goulston Street with another detective when he first heard about the writing and about the missing portion of the victim's apron. He stood guard over the writing for some considerable time while his companion (Detective Hunt) left to make arrangements for the writing to be photographed. Detective Halse copied down the message in his notebook but the message he recorded differed slightly from that recorded by PC Long. According to Halse, the message read, 'The Juwes are not the men that will be blamed for nothing.'

Halse's version is more likely to be the correct one because he spent a long time standing over the graffiti and staring at it. The writing was described as being 'in a good schoolboy hand' and was written in white chalk on the black fascia of a wall. Halse assumed that the writing had been recently done because there were a lot of people living in the tenement block and he believed it would have been erased if it had been there for any length of time.

Instead, the writing was erased on the orders of Sir Charles Warren (Commissioner of the Metropolitan Police), who was concerned about the possibility of anti-Jewish riots if the writing was allowed to remain on the wall. Warren was probably correct in his assessment of the situation: if the word had got around the East End that Jack the Ripper was a Jew, however flimsy the pretext, there would have been acts of violence committed against Jews. Warren's only mistake was that he panicked and ordered the writing to be erased at 5.30 a.m. before it had been photographed. With hindsight, it is easy to say that he should have allowed the writing to be photographed but that is to misunderstand the panic that was sweeping through London or the consequences for innocent Jews if the writing had become public knowledge. By 5.30 a.m., people were moving about and the discovery of the writing by the public was imminent. So Warren's actions are understandable. Also, with hindsight, it is hard to see how a photograph of some graffiti on a wall that was unrelated to the crime would have assisted the police investigation.

The theory has been put forward that Warren ordered the erasing of the graffiti because it implicated a high-ranking person. This theory implicates Warren in a cover-up in which the role of the police was to protect the identity of the murderer rather than expose it. The problem with the theory is that it is not obvious whom the graffiti was meant to implicate.

And again it is probable, if not certain, that Jews would have been at risk had the populace at large been allowed to read the graffiti. A lot of women had died without the police getting a sniff of the killer and people in general were panicking. The following two reports from *The Times* (12 November 1888) give an indication of the kind of mood that was sweeping through London:

> Great excitement was caused shortly before 10 o'clock last night by the arrest of a man with a blackened face who publicly proclaimed himself to be 'Jack the Ripper'. This was at the scene of the latest crime. Two young men, one a discharged soldier, immediately seized him, and the great crowd, which always on a Sunday night parades this neighbourhood, raised a cry of 'Lynch him.' Sticks were raised, the man was furiously attacked, and but for the timely arrival of the police he would have been seriously injured.

> Shortly after 10 o'clock last night as a woman named Humphreys was passing George Yard, Whitechapel, she met in the darkness . . . a powerful-looking man wearing large spectacles. Trembling with agitation she asked 'What do you want?' The man made no answer but

laughed and made a hasty retreat. The woman shouted 'murder' several times and soon alarmed the neighbours. Uniformed policeman and detectives ran to the yard from all directions. They entered a house into which the man had retreated, and he was apprehended. A crowd of people quickly collected, who exhibited an almost unanimous inclination to lynch the mysterious person, but the police were fortunately able to protect him.

By 5.30 a.m., a lot of people were awake and ready to make their way to work. If the rumour had got about that the last murder had something to do with the Jews, there can be no doubt as to the consequences. It should also be remembered that catching Jack the Ripper was only *one* part of Warren's job: he also had a responsibility to maintain public order and to prevent crimes before they were committed.

The body found in Mitre Square was identified as that of Catherine Eddowes. She was 46 years old and had been living with a man called John Kelly. She never married him but that did not stop her sometimes giving her name as Kate Kelly. Before she met Kelly, she had lived with a man called Thomas Conway and had three children by him.

But Thomas Conway was a teetotaller who strongly disapproved of his wife's drinking habits. Their relationship steadily deteriorated until Conway left her. At the time of her death, Eddowes had not lived with Conway for seven or eight years.

After her break-up with Conway, Eddowes got into the habit of visiting her daughter Annie and asking for money. Her two sons were still living with Conway but she did not know where to find them; their address had been purposely kept from her to stop her visiting and asking for money. At this time, her daughter Annie was living with a man named Phillips in King Street, Bermondsey. Annie seems to have viewed her mother as a nuisance or an embarrassment. The two women last saw each other in September 1886. Approximately one month later, Annie left King Street with her husband and did not leave a forwarding address.

Not long after her break-up with Conway, Eddowes fell in with John Kelly. Kelly was three years her junior and down on his luck. He had worked for a fruiterer for 12 years but was now reduced to wandering about the East End and taking what work he could get on a day-to-day basis. If a day went by without him getting any work, he would put something into pawn to get enough money for a bed and a bite to eat.

Eddowes did not live with Kelly in the conventional sense. Although they stuck together for seven years, they were never able to rent a room and live together as husband and wife. Instead, they had to rent a double bed in a common lodging house at 55 Flower and Dean Street at a cost of 8d. a night. Even so, they seemed to live happily together except on the few occasions when Eddowes got drunk. Eddowes herself was described as 'a very jolly woman' and often liked to sing.

Kelly last saw Eddowes at 2 p.m. on Saturday, 29 September. The last meal they had together was breakfast that morning. As usual, the couple had no money; in a very touching gesture, Kelly got the cash for breakfast by going to a pawnbroker and pawning his boots. He and Eddowes ate between 10 a.m. and 11 a.m. After breakfast, they had a chat about their desperate situation. Kelly suggested to Eddowes that she should visit her daughter to try to get the price of a bed for the night. Eddowes went off on a forlorn journey to Bermondsey to look for the daughter who was no longer there. She had promised Kelly that she would be back by 4 p.m. and they parted on the best of terms. When Kelly next saw Eddowes, her body was lying unrecognisable in the mortuary.

Eddowes had no money when she left Kelly and had gone to Bermondsey. She could not have found her daughter but must have got money from somewhere. By 8.30 p.m. Saturday, she had found enough cash to drink herself into a stupor.

PC Louis Robinson was on duty in Aldgate High Street when he came upon Eddowes lying semi-conscious in the street and smelling strongly of drink. Another constable arrived shortly afterwards and, together, they took Eddowes to Bishopsgate Police Station, where she was put in a cell till she sobered up.

Constable George Hutt, who was the gaoler inside the police station, visited Eddowes in her cell once every half hour. She was sound asleep when he started his shift at 9.45 p.m. and had already been in her cell for an hour. At 12.15 a.m., she was awake and singing to herself. When he took a look at her at 12.30 a.m., she asked when she was going to be let out and Hutt replied, 'When you are capable of taking care of yourself.' She answered that she was capable of taking care of herself there and then.

Hutt seems to have believed her because he let her out of the cell at 12.58 a.m. after Sergeant Byfield had told him to see if there were any prisoners fit for discharge. As Hutt was bringing Eddowes out of her cell, she asked him the time. 'Too late for you to get any more drink,' he told her. She asked him again and this time he told her that it was 'Just on one.' Eddowes then said, 'I shall get a damned fine hiding when I get home.'

However, she does not seem to have gone straight home. With Kelly having pawned his boots to get breakfast for her, she may have felt that she could not go back to the lodging house without at least getting some money. At about 1.35 a.m., she was seen with a man at the corner of Church passage, which led from Duke Street into Mitre Square.

The witnesses, who were the last people to see Eddowes alive, were Joseph Lawende and Joseph Hyam Levy. They had been drinking at the Imperial Club in Duke Street. Lawende glanced at Eddowes and noticed that she was with a man who was wearing a cloth cap with a peak. Eddowes had put her hand on the man's chest. Levy, though, did not stare at the couple. He saw them but paid them very little attention. His only impression was that the man was three or four inches taller than the woman. He walked on down Duke Street, into Aldgate, leaving them talking together.

It is interesting to note that one witness had also seen Elizabeth Stride with a man who wore a peaked cap like a sailor's.

The following day, a curious incident occurred in Whitechapel Road. Thomas Coram lived at 67 Plummer's Road, Mile End, and was employed in a coconut warehouse. About 24 hours after the murder, he was coming away from friends at 16 Bath Gardens, Brady Street, and was walking up Whitechapel Road towards Aldgate when he saw a knife lying on the doorstep of No. 252 (Coram had just crossed over from No. 253).

The building at No. 252 was a laundry and had two steps leading up to the front door. The knife was on the bottom step. A handkerchief had been folded and wrapped around the handle and Coram could see what looked like bloodstains on the handkerchief. The blade was dagger-shaped and sharpened on one side. It was also nine or ten inches long. Dr Phillips, after the post-mortem of Annie Chapman, had said that the killer had used a very sharp knife at least six to eight inches long and probably longer.

Constable Joseph Drage was on fixed duty in Whitechapel Road that night. At about 12.30 a.m. on Monday morning, he saw Coram stopping in a doorway opposite No. 253. Coram then stood up and beckoned to him, saying, 'Policeman, there is a knife down there.' PC Drage shone his lantern over the spot and saw the knife. It was covered in dried blood and the handkerchief was bound around the handle and tied with string.

The knife may have been there for less than 15 minutes. PC Drage had passed that spot several times that night and had not noticed it. Most certainly, it was not there an hour previously when the landlady let a woman out of the laundry.

PC Drage remembered going over to help when a horse fell down at that very spot. It seemed highly probable that the owner had thrown the knife away at that moment.

Why would an innocent man be carrying a bloodstained knife in his hand? And if the man was innocent, why should he throw the knife away on the approach of a policeman? Surely it was also an extraordinary coincidence that the bloodstained knife was very similar to the instrument used on Annie Chapman?

This incident is potentially significant. If the man who threw the knife away was Jack the Ripper, then it means that Jack the Ripper owned a horse. There is no description of the horse and we do not know why it fell: it may, for example, have stumbled on a loose cobblestone. But William Bury, it should be remembered, owned a pony that took ill with the glanders.

Another strange incident occurred only a few hours later and may throw some light on the Ripper's ability to disappear from the scenes of his crimes. Here is the incident as reported in *The Times* on 2 October 1888:

> Yesterday evening a singular discovery, which is supposed to afford an important clue to the murderer, was being investigated by the police in Kentish Town. At about 9 o'clock in the morning the proprietor of the Nelson Tavern, Victoria Road, Kentish Town, entered a place of convenience adjoining his premises for the purpose of pointing out to a builder some alterations which he

desired executed, when a paper parcel was noticed behind the door. No particular importance was attached to the discovery until an hour later, when Mr Chinn, the publican, while reading the newspaper, was struck with the similarity of this bundle to the one which the police had issued a description as having been in the possession of the man last seen in the company with the woman Stride. The police at the Kentish Town Road Police Station were told of the discovery and a detective officer was at once sent to make inquiries. It was then found that the parcel, which had been kicked into the roadway, contained a pair of dark trousers. The description of the man wanted on suspicion of having committed the murders gives the colour of the trousers he wore as dark. The paper which contained the trousers was stained with blood.

Had the killer taken a change of clothes with him, wrapped in a newspaper parcel? Had he changed quickly, in a dark corner, and wrapped up his bloodstained trousers in the newspaper parcel? Had breathless police officers rushed past him, looking in vain for a man with blood on his clothes?

We cannot say that these trousers were discarded by Jack the Ripper. But suppose, for a moment, that the trousers were owned by an innocent man who worked in an abattoir. What reason would he have for discarding them in the public place?

This discovery poses other questions. The man was not carrying a spare pair of trousers by accident. He knew he was going to get his trousers covered in blood and he knew he would have to change out of them because he did not want to be walking through the streets with blood on his clothes.

At the very least, we must consider it a strong possibility that Jack the Ripper carried spare clothes on his person on the nights of the murders and changed out of his bloodstained clothes as he made his escape. We cannot be certain that the newspaper parcel was the same one that PC Smith saw but it does mean that the man seen by Smith must be considered a strong suspect.

16

JEKYLL, HYDE AND JACK THE RIPPER

SIX WOMEN WERE DEAD BY NOW, AT LEAST FOUR OF THEM BY the hand of Jack the Ripper.

But something else was happening in London that would dominate the investigation into the crimes of Jack the Ripper for more than a century. In 1886, Robert Louis Stevenson wrote the classic horror story *The Strange Case of Dr Jekyll and Mr Hyde*. What particularly horrified the readers of Victorian Britain was the book's depiction of the triumph of evil over good: it is the respectable Dr Jekyll who is destroyed by the devils within him which take the shape of Mr Hyde.

The evil Hyde is not a separate person from Jekyll; he is merely released when Jekyll takes a potion. The story may be an allegory about the way in which alcohol or drugs can bring about undesired changes in the personality of the individual. But it is also an allegory about the duality of the human persona: evil lurks within us all. Hyde is a part of Jekyll's persona: a part so powerful that, in the end, Jekyll is destroyed.

In perhaps the worst piece of timing in the history of the theatre, *Dr Jekyll and Mr Hyde* commenced its run at London's Lyceum Theatre on 4 August 1888. Performances began at 8.15 each evening. Although based on Stevenson's famous book, the play itself was written by T. Russell Sullivan and starred the famous American actor Richard Mansfield.

On 6 August – the same day that Martha Tabram was murdered – *The Times* published the following review of the new show:

In view of the very considerable stir made by the rival adapters of 'The Strange Case of Dr Jekyll and Mr Hyde', it is possible that the public may have formed an exaggerated idea both of the dramatic merits of that work and of the power with which the dual personality of the central character is, or can be, presented on the stage . . . There is but little scope for acting in what has been described as Mr Stevenson's 'psychological study' . . . There is no transfusion of thought or character between 'Dr Jekyll' and 'Mr Hyde.' In look, dress, and action they are wholly distinct individuals; and Mr Mansfield's appearance, now in one part and now in the other involve no more psychology than the 'business' of a 'quick-change artiste' in the music halls . . . The play is thus reduced to a mere string of episodes in connexion [sic] with the dual character of its hero. First Dr Jekyll appears; next Mr Hyde; then, after the metamorphosis has occurred a few times behind the scenes, Mr Hyde changes into Dr Jekyll under the eye of the house but with 'lights down', when he mixes and drinks his mysterious powders in Dr Lanyon's study; finally Dr Jekyll involuntarily falls back into the repulsive shape of Mr Hyde . . . takes poison and dies. Instead of trying to preserve or to suggest the identity of the two men in their different shapes, Mr Mansfield . . . presents them as different characters, Dr Jekyll being a bland and somewhat platitudinous philanthropist, who has a tendency to grope with his right hand in the region of his heart, while Mr Hyde is a crouching Quilp-like creature, a malignant Quasimodo, who hisses and snorts like a wild beast. As Dr Jekyll, Mr Mansfield does not strike one as an actor of remarkable resource; as Mr Hyde, however, he plays with a rough vigour or power which, allied to his hideous aspect, thrills the house, producing a sensation composed in equal measure of the morbidly fascinating and the downright disagreeable. Studies of the horrible are not usually attractive to the public who, after all, go to the theatre mainly for the purpose of being pleasantly entertained and lifted out of themselves. The truth of this axiom playwrights have more than once found to their cost. Still *The Strange Case of Dr Jekyll and Mr Hyde* appeals in a certain degree to a love of the occult which is deeply implanted in the human mind, and it may for that reason be able to hold its place in the Lyceum bill.

On 30 August, Polly Nichols was murdered. On 7 September, Annie Chapman was murdered. By 17 September, Richard Mansfield's performance was attracting some extraordinary reviews. 'He has come, he has been seen, he has conquered,' claimed the *Daily Telegraph*. 'Intensely powerful,' said the *Saturday Review*. 'Stirred the audience deeply,' commented the *Sunday Times*. But already audiences were dwindling. The theatre-going public seemed to have lost its appetite for horror: there were, perhaps, enough monsters lurking out-of-doors.

On 17 September, there was a re-scheduling. *Dr Jekyll and Mr Hyde* would now begin at the later time of 9 p.m. so that it could be preceded by *Lesbia*, 'a classical comedy in one act'. *Lesbia*, with Beatrice Cameron in the title role, commenced at 8 p.m.

The double murder of Elizabeth Stride and Catherine Eddowes occurred on 30 September. On 1 October, *Dr Jekyll and Mr Hyde* prematurely ended its run at the Lyceum and was replaced by the comedy *A Parisien Romance*, with Richard Mansfield quickly learning the lines for the part of Baron Chevrial.

But *A Parisien Romance* was not a success. On 13 October, the Lyceum tried to bring back *Dr Jekyll and Mr Hyde*, supported once more by the comedy *Lesbia*. This time, *Jekyll and Hyde* lasted only one week before being taken off again. By 22 October, Richard Mansfield was treading the boards at the Lyceum in *Prince Karl*, a comedy by Archibald Gunter.

By a quirk of fate, the story of the placid Dr Jekyll transforming into the demonic Mr Hyde had emerged at a time when there was a real-life demon stalking the streets of London. Perhaps inevitably, Dr Jekyll and Jack the Ripper became intertwined in the public consciousness. A lot of the elements of the Jekyll and Hyde story became the template for Ripper investigation. Everything that Jack the Ripper might be is personified by Dr Jekyll: he is a 'respectable' man from the West End of London who is leading a double life at night. He commits murder because he enjoys it and then reverts to his daytime persona of Jekyll, whom no one would ever suspect.

Many of the conspiracy theories about the concealment of the identity of Jack the Ripper by the authorities owe their origin to

Stevenson's *Jekyll and Hyde*. Because Jekyll is losing control in his own personal battle of wills, he takes his own life. He cannot defeat Hyde and, therefore, in a moment of lucidity, he takes his own life to put a stop to Hyde's reign of terror. In effect, Jekyll kills himself to stop his other identity as Hyde being discovered by the authorities. He kills himself to protect his own good name and his friends collude in this conspiracy.

What is the most popular image we have today of Jack the Ripper? That he was a West Ender, possibly a doctor, and that there has been a cover-up to protect the name of the perpetrator. Thus, the name of the perpetrator was known to a select group of eminent Victorians who lived in the West End of London and who maintained a wall of silence to protect the good name of the individual.

Although it was fiction, the Jekyll and Hyde story was so powerful that we have taken it and transplanted it onto a series of true crimes – the crimes of Jack the Ripper. The popular suspects clearly fit the 'Dr Jekyll' label:

- Montague John Druitt – a barrister, educated at Oxford;
- William Gladstone – Prime Minister;
- Sir William Gull – physician to Queen Victoria;
- Dr Pedachenko – a doctor working for the Russian Secret Service;
- Prince Albert, Duke of Clarence – grandson of Queen Victoria;
- Lord Salisbury – Prime Minister;
- Walter Sickert – a famous British artist;
- Dr Stanley – a brilliant doctor with a large aristocratic practice.

This is an illustrious list which contains three doctors, two Prime Ministers and the grandson of Queen Victoria. All of these suspects fit the Jekyll template. But all of this is more akin to the world of detective fiction than true crime. Not one of these so-called suspects is *known* to have killed anyone (under any circumstances). If we are to postulate that either Sir William Gull or Walter Sickert, for example, were responsible for the crimes of Jack the Ripper, then it becomes essential to demonstrate a capability on the part of either man to commit gruesome murder.

More than a century later, it is possible to accuse any eminent Victorian of the crimes. There cannot be a trial and the accused cannot speak up for himself. Only the thinnest, most insubstantial evidence need be offered up by the accuser.

But a motive on the part of the accuser also needs to be considered. More than one book has speculated that the Victorian artist Walter Sickert was connected to the murders. The immediate effect of this is to generate interest in Sickert and ensure that the value of his paintings goes up. To those galleries or individuals who hold paintings of Sickert's, the publicity attaching his name to the crimes of Jack the Ripper is a positive boon. It does not matter that there is absolutely no evidence that Sickert had either the inclination or the ability to commit Ripper-type murders. Take a wild theory about Jack the Ripper, however improbable, throw in royalty, freemasons or even a black magician and you may have the makings of a bestseller. But this is a long way from the real detectives who hunted Jack the Ripper, who had to find some real evidence that would not only lead them to the killer but could also be presented to a court where it would have to withstand cross-examination by Her Majesty's Counsel for the Defence.

17

MARY JANE KELLY

MARY JANE KELLY LIVED IN A ROOM AT 13 MILLER'S COURT. SHE rented the room from John McCarthy, who also owned a chandler's shop in the neighbouring Dorset Street. By Friday, 9 November 1888, Kelly was 29s. behind with her rent (the rent was 4s.6d. a week). At 10.45 on Friday morning, McCarthy told Thomas Bowyer, who worked in the shop, to go to No. 13 to try to get some rent.

Bowyer went to Miller's Court and knocked on the door of No. 13. When there was no reply, he tried the door handle but found that the door had been locked. He then looked through the keyhole and noticed that the key was missing.

Next to the door was a window with a broken pane of glass. Bowyer put his hand through the broken pane and pulled aside the muslin curtain that covered it. The first thing he saw were two lumps of flesh lying on the table by the bed. Then his eyes fell upon the remains of Kelly – naked, dead and covered in blood.

Bowyer ran back to tell McCarthy, who decided to take a look for himself. As he explained to *The Times*:

> The sight I saw was more ghastly than even I had prepared myself for. On the bed lay the body as my man had told me, while the table was covered with what seemed to me to be lumps of flesh.

McCarthy told Bowyer not to say a word about the murder to any of the neighbours but to rush straight to Commercial Road Police Station.

Police officers arrived but none of them seemed to know what to do. Inspector Beck then came, followed by Inspector Abberline, Dr Phillips and Superintendent Arnold. Inspector Abberline gave orders that no one should be allowed to enter or leave the court. At about 11.15 a.m., Dr Phillips arrived. He looked through the window and told everyone what they already knew – that Mary Jane Kelly was dead. Superintendent Arnold ordered that one of the windows should be removed so that everyone could get a better look at the mess.

A telegram was dispatched to Sir Charles Warren, asking him to send bloodhounds so they could track down the murderer by following his scent. But no one seemed to know that Sir Charles Warren had resigned following criticism of the investigation by the newspapers, and so they spent the next two hours waiting.

But what would bloodhounds have been able to do? The killer's scent was in Mary Jane Kelly's room – but where, exactly? Kelly's scent was also going to be all over the room along with the scent of anyone else who had recently been inside.

A bloodhound can only track a suspect or fugitive if it knows which scent to follow and the police only had one item which they knew had been handled by Jack the Ripper – the portion of Catherine Eddowes's apron. But given that Eddowes had been wearing the apron and that it was soaked with her blood, her smells would also be on it.

But the bloodhounds never arrived. By the time Superintendent Arnold eventually ordered the door to be broken down, the police had lost two hours of potentially valuable time. They arrived on the scene shortly after 11 a.m. but the door was not broken down till approximately 1 p.m.

It was John McCarthy who broke down the door and here we pick up his story:

> I at once forced the door with a pickaxe and we entered the room. The sight we saw I cannot drive away from my mind. It looked more like the work of a devil than of a man. The poor woman's body was lying on the bed, undressed. She had been completely disembowelled, and her entrails had been taken out and placed on the table. It was those that I had seen when I looked through the window and took to be lumps of flesh. The woman's nose had been cut off, and her face gashed and mutilated so

that she was quite beyond recognition. Both her breasts
too had been cut clean away and placed by the side of her
liver and other entrails on the table. I had heard a great
deal about the Whitechapel murders, but I declare to God
I had never expected to see such a sight as this. The body
was, of course, covered with blood, and so was the bed.
The whole scene is more than I can describe. I hope I never
see such a scene again.

Mary Jane Kelly lay on her back, naked apart from the remains
of a chemise. Her throat had been cut from ear to ear and was
severed all the way down to the spinal column. The ears and
nose had been cut clean off. The breasts had also been sliced off
and put on the table next to the bed. The stomach and abdomen
had been ripped open and the face had been repeatedly slashed
until the girl's features became unrecognisable. The kidneys had
been cut out of the body and put on the table next to the breasts.
The lower parts of the body and the uterus had been cut out and
even the thighs were cut. The heart was missing.

Kelly's clothes were lying by the side of the bed in a neat pile.
It looked as though she had taken them off and put them there
herself. They did not appear to have been cut off or torn off by
the murderer. It therefore appeared as if Kelly had voluntarily
undressed in front of her killer.

When the police forced open the door, it knocked against the
table which was close to the left-hand side of the bedstead. The
men then cautiously entered the room. It was a very poorly
furnished room, containing only an old bedstead, two tables and
a chair. It was also a very small room, being only 12 ft square.

Something curious was found in the fireplace. Amongst the
ashes, under a kettle, were the wirework of a woman's felt hat
and a piece of velvet. It seemed that an extremely fierce fire had
been burning during the night, because the handle and spout of
the kettle had actually been burnt off. However, a little bit of
caution is required here because it is not known when the
damage was done to the kettle.

Nevertheless, it did seem as if the killer had been burning
evidence in the fireplace. Inspector Abberline took a slightly
different view, believing that the clothes were burned so that the
Ripper could see what he was doing. Other police officers were of
the opinion that the murder had been committed in daylight

and the bloodstained articles had been burned in the fire. This theory was supported by the fact that the candle Mary Jane Kelly bought on Wednesday was found only half consumed. But the problem with this theory was that articles of clothing which were being pulled off the corpse soaked in blood would be damp and would tend to smoulder rather than burn.

At 3.50 p.m. a horse-driven cart with an ordinary tarpaulin cover was driven into Dorset Street and halted opposite Miller's Court. In *The Ripper File* by Elwyn Jones and John Lloyd, it is reported that the entrance to Miller's Court was only 3 ft wide. The cart was obviously too wide to get into the court. A long shell or coffin, dirty and scratched from constant use, was taken from the cart and carried inside.

News that the body was about to be taken went around the court and a great rush of people came hurrying out of the side streets around Dorset Street. The crowds were soon pressing around the cart and some men were seen doffing their caps and some women shedding tears. The coffin was covered with a ragged-looking cloth and loaded on to the cart. The body was taken to Shoreditch Mortuary.

The scene of the crime was a small, poverty-stricken court containing only seven houses. Kelly's room had originally been the back parlour of 26 Dorset Street but a partition had been erected and then a door was put in facing Miller's Court. Both Dorset Street and Miller's Court housed only society's losers, whether they stayed in tiny rooms or in doss houses. *The Times* remarked that such was the poverty of the neighbourhood that 'nearly the whole of the houses in the street are common lodging houses and the one opposite where this murder was enacted has accommodation for some 300 men and is fully occupied every night'.

The inquest into the death of Mary Jane Kelly was conducted by Dr Roderick MacDonald. It was unlike any of the other inquests and was over almost before it had begun. Coroner MacDonald surprisingly brought it to a close before all the witnesses had been called and before the time of death had been established. He justified this by saying that it was in the interests of justice not to disclose certain details about the death of Mary Jane Kelly. In *A Casebook on Jack the Ripper*, Richard Whittington-Egan speculated that the police had some evidence which they wished to keep to themselves so as not to put the killer on his guard. He went on to make the interesting suggestion that they had found semen in Mary Jane Kelly's rectum. The police, however, were never given the opportunity to follow this lead up: Jack the Ripper never struck again in London.

The murder of Mary Jane Kelly was the most unusual of the five Jack the Ripper murders. It was the only one committed indoors and was also the only one carried out on a young and beautiful woman. At 25 years old, Mary Jane Kelly was about 20 years younger than the other victims.

It was reported in the press that Kelly had been born in Limerick but emigrated to Wales while she was still quite young because her father got a job at an ironworks either in Carmarthen or Caernarvon. She married a collier named Davis when she was 16 and lived with him till he was killed in an explosion a year or two afterwards. She moved to Cardiff and then moved to London in 1884. She is said to have lived in a 'gay house' in the West End. In Victorian London, a gay house would have had nothing to do with homosexuality but would, most likely, have been a high-class brothel. After that, she went to France with a gentleman but returned soon afterwards because she did not like it. She then lived with a man called Morganstone in Ratcliff Highway and later lived with a man named Joseph Fleming in Bethnal Green.

The last man that Kelly lived with was a man called Joseph Barnett. He met her in Spitalfields one Friday night and arranged to meet her again the next day. Begg, Fido and Skinner, in *The Jack the Ripper A–Z*, give the date of this encounter as 8 April 1887. Very soon, Barnett and Kelly had agreed to live together. They had several addresses in the East End, eventually settling at Miller's Court. It was Kelly, not Barnett, who rented the room. Somehow or other, they ran up a debt of 29s. About ten days before her death, Kelly had a violent quarrel with Barnett. The circumstances surrounding this quarrel were very strange.

According to Barnett, he and Kelly lived happily together until another woman – Maria Harvey – moved in with them. Not surprisingly, perhaps, Barnett objected to this very strongly. After putting up with Harvey for two or three nights, Barnett quarrelled with Kelly and moved out. The quarrel was so violent that blows were exchanged and a window pane was broken.

This sequence of events provoked a series of questions. Who was the woman Maria Harvey? What was she doing in Kelly's room? Why did this result in a quarrel between Kelly and Barnett? Perhaps the most logical explanation for these events has been put forward by Donald Rumbelow in *The Complete Jack the Ripper*. Rumbelow's theory is that McCarthy was a racketeer controlling a number of prostitutes, of whom Mary Jane Kelly was one.

Rumbelow argues that McCarthy put Maria Harvey – another prostitute – into 13 Miller's Court to disrupt Barnett's life with Kelly and force him out of the room. Barnett had been keeping Kelly off the streets and, by forcing him out, McCarthy no doubt intended to get Kelly back into prostitution. Rumbelow's conclusion is that McCarthy had allowed Kelly to run up a debt of 29s. to give him a hold over her.

Barnett went to live in Buller's common lodging house in Bishopsgate Street. Kelly was now forced to support herself by walking the streets. Maria Harvey, her task accomplished, now moved out but Barnett did not return. However, he visited Kelly regularly and often gave her money. On Thursday, 8 November, he visited her between 7.30 p.m. and 8 p.m., and apologised to her because he had no money to give her.

The next sighting we have of Kelly is in Commercial Street at approximately 11.30 p.m., when she was alone and making her way home. Fifteen minutes later, at 11.45 p.m., she was seen with a man in Miller's Court by Mary Ann Cox – a widow who also lived in Miller's Court and had turned to prostitution to make ends meet. Kelly was intoxicated and the man she was with was short, stout, shabbily dressed and wore a round billycock hat. He had a blotchy face and a heavy carroty moustache, and was carrying a pot of beer. Cox followed them into the court and said goodnight to Kelly, who replied, 'Goodnight; I am going to sing.' The man who was with her was wearing dark clothes and looked about 35 or 36 years old.

Cox heard Kelly's door being shut and then heard her singing the popular song 'Only a violet I plucked from my mother's grave'. Cox went back to her room for 15 minutes and noticed that Kelly was still singing when she came out again. Cox did not return till 3.10 a.m. By then, Kelly's light was off and there was no noise coming from her room. Cox went to bed but was unable to sleep. She heard a man leave the court at 6.15 a.m.

George Hutchinson was the next person to see Mary Jane Kelly. He was a labourer who knew her either as a customer or as a friend or both. He gave a very detailed description to the police, which was published in the newspapers and ran as follows:

> At two o'clock on Friday morning, I came down Whitechapel Road into Commercial Street. As I passed Thrawl Street I passed a man standing at the corner of the street, and as I went towards Flower and Dean Street I met the woman Kelly whom I knew very well, having been in her company a number of times. She said, 'Mr Hutchinson, can you lend me sixpence?' I said I could not. She then walked towards Thrawl Street, saying she must go and look for some money. The man who was standing at the corner of Thrawl Street then came towards her and put his hand on her shoulder and said something to her, which I did not hear, and they both burst out laughing. He put his hand again on her shoulder and they both walked slowly towards me. I walked on to the corner of Fashion Street, near the public house. As they came by me, his arm was still on her shoulder. He had a soft felt hat on and this was drawn down somewhat over his eyes. I put down my head to look him in the face, and he turned and looked at me very sternly, and they walked across the road to Dorset Street. They stood at the corner of Miller's Court for about three minutes. Kelly spoke to the man in a loud voice, saying, 'I have lost my handkerchief.' He pulled a red handkerchief out of his pocket and gave it to Kelly, and they both went up the court together. I went to look up the court to see if I could see them, but could not. I stood there for three-quarters of an hour, to see if they came down again, but they did not, and so I went away. My suspicions were aroused by seeing the man so well dressed but I had no suspicion that he was the murderer. The man was about 5 ft 6 in. in height and 34 or 35 years of age, with dark complexion and dark moustache turned up at the ends. He was wearing a long dark coat trimmed with astrakhan, a white collar with black necktie, in which was affixed a horse-shoe pin. He wore a pair of dark spats with light buttons over buttoned boots, and displayed from his waistcoat a massive gold chain. His watch chain had a big seal with a red stone hanging from it. He had a heavy

moustache curled up, and dark eyes and bushy eyebrows. He had no side whiskers, and his chin was clean shaven. He looked like a foreigner. I went up to the court and stayed there a couple of minutes, but did not see any light in the house or hear any noise. I was out last night until three o'clock looking for him. I could swear to the man anywhere. The man I saw carried a small parcel in his hand about eight inches long and it had a strap around it. He had it tightly grasped in his left hand. It looked as though it was covered with dark American cloth. He carried in his right hand, which he had laid upon the woman's shoulder, a pair of brown kid gloves . . . Kelly did not seem to me to be drunk, but was a little spreeish.

George Hutchinson gave up his vigil shortly before 3 a.m. At that time, the well-dressed man was still in Kelly's room.

The description Hutchinson gives of Kelly's client is extraordinarily detailed, for someone he passed in a dark street. We have no reason to disbelieve Hutchinson and he does not seem to have had a motive to lie about the encounter. The only reason he would invent a story like this would be to protect someone else but this is unlikely because Hutchinson seems to be someone who had feelings for Kelly.

In his statement, Hutchinson says, 'I met the woman Kelly whom I knew very well, having been in her company a number of times.' Kelly says to him, 'Mr Hutchinson, can you lend me sixpence?'

Hutchinson admits to knowing Kelly 'very well' and says he has often been in her company. Yet Kelly addresses him not as 'George' but as 'Mr Hutchinson'. If they were friends, why were they not on first-name terms? The only possible explanation is that Hutchinson was a client of Kelly's.

That may explain Hutchinson's intense interest in the man he saw with Kelly. If he had developed feelings for Kelly, he may have been unhappy that she was taking another man home. Hutchinson also seems to have decided that the man he saw was the murderer. His attention was drawn towards a well-dressed man he saw with Kelly but he said, 'I had no suspicion that he was the murderer.'

There is some evidence to suggest that the man Hutchinson saw may have been the murderer. This evidence comes from

Elizabeth Prater who lived at 20 Miller's Court. Her room was described as being 'just over Kelly's', which presumably meant she had the room above Kelly. Prater could usually hear Kelly moving about. On the night of the murder, she was disturbed by a kitten in her room at about 3.30 a.m. or 4 a.m. Soon afterwards, she heard a cry of 'Oh, murder.' The cry was in a female voice and seemed to come from the court. However, cries of 'murder' were common in the court and so Prater took no notice and went back to sleep.

Together, the evidence of George Hutchinson and Elizabeth Prater seems to indicate that Kelly may have been murdered between 3.30 and 4 a.m. by the man seen by Hutchinson. However, this evidence is completely contradicted by one of the other witnesses who testified at the inquest – Caroline Maxwell.

Caroline Maxwell lived at 14 Dorset Street and was the wife of Henry Maxwell, a lodging house deputy. She said that she saw Kelly between 8 a.m. and 8.30 a.m. on Friday morning.

Mrs Maxwell stated that she saw Kelly at the corner of Miller's Court and was sure about the time because it was the time her husband finished work. She was surprised to see Kelly up and about at that early hour and went over to speak to her. She asked Kelly what she was doing out of bed and Kelly said to her, 'I can't sleep. I have the horrors from drink.' Mrs Maxwell then asked Kelly to have a drink with her – a strange suggestion unless Mrs Maxwell was thinking that a hair of the dog might cure Kelly's hangover.

Kelly refused, saying that she was ill and had just had a half pint of ale which she brought up again. Mrs Maxwell then left Kelly and went into Bishopsgate Street to do some shopping. When she returned about half an hour later, she saw Kelly talking to a short, dark man. The time was between 8.30 a.m. and 9 a.m.

Therefore, there are two approximate times of death: about 4 a.m. and sometime after 9 a.m. on Friday morning. Obviously, only one of these can be correct. As with the other murders, the killer seems to have vanished into thin air. It is true that Dorset Street was a street made up mainly of common lodging houses and that all kinds of people could be found walking along it at all hours of the night. It was the kind of street where strangers would not have been noticed. Nevertheless, given the state that Kelly was found in, the murderer's clothes must have been covered in blood. It is surely remarkable that the killer was able to leave her room and walk away unnoticed.

It was reported in the newspapers that a man with a black bag was seen in the vicinity of Miller's Court both before and after the murder. On Wednesday, 6 November, a 20-year-old girl called Sarah Roney was with two other girls in Brushfield Street, which was near Dorset Street, when they were approached by a man wearing a tall hat and black coat. The man was carrying a black bag and he came up to Roney and said, 'Will you come with me?' She told him she would not and asked him what he had in the bag. He answered, 'Something the ladies don't like,' and then walked away.

The following report also appeared in *The Times* on Saturday, 10 November:

> A Mrs Paumier, a young woman who sells roasted chestnuts at the corner of Widegate Street, a narrow thoroughfare about two minutes' walk from the scene of the murder, told a reporter yesterday afternoon a story which appears to afford a clue to the murderer. She said that about 12 o'clock that morning a man dressed like a gentleman came to her and said, 'I suppose you have heard about the murder in Dorset Street?' She that she had, whereupon the man grinned, and said, 'I know more about it than you.' He then stared into her face and went down Sandy's Row, another narrow thoroughfare which cuts across Widegate Street. When he got some way off, however, he looked back as if to see whether she was watching him, and then vanished. Mrs Paumier said that the man had a black moustache, was about 5 ft 6 in high, and wore a black silk hat, a black coat, and speckled trousers. He also carried a black shiny bag about a foot in depth and a foot and a half in length.

The problem with newspaper reports like these is that the black shiny bag was probably a Gladstone bag, named after W.E. Gladstone, who was Prime Minister for 14 years between 1868 and 1894. A Gladstone bag would not have been uncommon in London in 1888. The murderer may have carried one – but so would countless other men.

The murder of Mary Jane Kelly seems to have thrown up a few

mysteries which have fuelled the imaginations of the conspiracy theorists. The first mystery concerns the roaring fire. What was the killer burning in the fireplace and why did he need such a blazing fire?

There is also the mystery of the missing key. The key to Kelly's room had been missing for two weeks. But when McCarthy discovered the body, he found the door locked and had to break it down with a pickaxe. This suggests that the killer had had the key and had locked the door as he made his escape. The next logical conclusion to draw is that the killer knew Kelly; that he had stolen the key sometime previously and returned with it on the night he intended to kill her.

And the next logical conclusion we must draw is that the killing of Mary Jane Kelly was not a random murder but was premeditated. And then it becomes clear what the killer was burning in the fireplace: evidence that connected him to Kelly.

But all of this may be a wild-goose chase. Kelly could bolt the door from the inside. And there was a way of making it look like the door was locked when she was out of her room. The window pane next to the door was broken and she was in the habit of locking it by putting her hand through the broken window pane and drawing the bolt. The killer would have seen her do this as he entered her room and would have been able to lock it in similar manner as he left.

In *A Casebook on Jack the Ripper*, Richard Whittington-Egan made the simple suggestion that neither John McCarthy nor Thomas Bowyer knew about the bolt. That means John McCarthy broke the door down with a pickaxe because he thought the door was locked and did not know it was merely bolted. On trying the door handle, he had assumed that it was locked because he did not know Kelly had lost her key. He therefore thought the key was inside the room and that a forced means of entry was necessary.

And the blazing fire can also be explained in a similarly mundane manner. It was November: with a broken window, it would have been cold and draughty in the room. Kelly would have been burning material in the fireplace simply to keep warm. If a cold draught was coming in through the window, she might have needed to build up a big fire.

Another mystery concerns the truncated inquest. The inquest into the death of Mary Jane Kelly was the shortest of the five inquests and was brought to a close by Coroner MacDonald before all the witnesses had testified. This has fuelled speculation that MacDonald was participating in a cover-up and was deliberately concealing evidence that might have implicated a VIP if it had been made available.

However, it was equally likely that MacDonald took the view that an examination of Kelly's gruesome injuries would serve no purpose other than to increase the state of public panic in the city. MacDonald did establish the cause of death, although that was rather obvious. And it is not clear what advantage the police would have gained from an extended inquiry. MacDonald brought his inquiry to an end before he heard George Hutchinson's evidence but we have to assume that Hutchinson's evidence was made available to the police. And since Hutchinson also made statements to the newspapers, the police could not have been unaware of his evidence. It may also be the case that MacDonald took advice from the police before he truncated the inquest: it may have been the police who did not want the full details of Kelly's murder to be made public.

The one thing that Coroner MacDonald did not establish beyond reasonable doubt was the time of death. We therefore have two possibilities: it occurred about 4 a.m. or it occurred about 9 a.m. The evidence for the '4 a.m. Scenario' runs as follows:

- George Hutchinson saw Mary Jane Kelly take a man back to her room at about 2 a.m. The man was still there three-quarters of an hour later and no one knows at what time he left;
- Elizabeth Prater heard a cry of 'Oh, murder' in Miller's Court at about 3.30 a.m. or 4 a.m.;
- Mary Ann Cox heard a man leave Miller's Court at about 6.15 a.m.

At first sight, this appears quite logical but a further examination of this evidence throws up serious problems. The first problem is the evidence of Elizabeth Prater. Prater lived in the room above Kelly and usually heard Kelly moving about in her room. If Kelly had screamed 'Murder!', then Prater would have heard the scream coming up through the floorboards under her feet. She would have known exactly where the cry came from and who made it. She would also – almost certainly – have recognised Kelly's voice.

But Elizabeth Prater did not know where the cry of 'Murder' came from, other than the fact that it was made by someone in Miller's Court. And yet, to repeat, such cries were common in the court and Prater ignored it because she had grown used to such disturbances. There is, therefore, nothing in Prater's evidence to suggest that it was Kelly who cried out that night.

In fact, Prater's evidence very strongly suggests that Kelly was not murdered at 4 a.m. It is reasonable to conclude that, if something had happened in Kelly's room at that time, Prater would have heard it. And if a cry or any other sound had come from Kelly's room, it would have been obvious to Prater exactly where the sound had come from.

There are other problems with the '4 a.m. Scenario'. It simply does not fit with what we know about Jack the Ripper. Whoever Jack the Ripper was, he was a man who worked quickly. Nichols, Chapman, Stride and Eddowes were all killed in very short spaces of time – and they had to be before the next policeman on the beat came along.

But the '4 a.m. Scenario' creates a picture of a killer who takes a lot of time to stalk and then kill his victims. The man seen by George Hutchinson met Mary Jane Kelly at 2 a.m. If he was the killer, it means he spent two hours with his victim before killing her at 4 a.m. He then spent another two hours disembowelling the body and destroying evidence in the fire before leaving at 6.15 a.m.

And if the '4 a.m. Scenario' is correct, the evidence of Caroline Maxwell must be wrong. But Mrs Maxwell had no motive to lie to the inquest. There is no reason to dispute her evidence beyond the possibility that she may have made an honest mistake.

Mrs Maxwell's evidence creates a problem for all those writers who have accepted without question the 'Dr Jekyll' hypothesis. In this hypothesis, the killer must work at night like Mr Hyde and cannot still be out on the streets in the daylight hours when he risks being discovered. By 9 a.m., he must have returned to his daytime 'Dr Jekyll' persona. Whether he is a lawyer, doctor or MP, he is someone who will be missed from his place of work if he is absent. He must be back at his desk by 9 a.m., which means his work must be done under cover of darkness.

In *Jack the Ripper: The Final Solution*, Stephen Knight states that

Mrs Maxwell was either lying, drunk or mistaken. Knight's problem is that her evidence contradicts his elaborate theory about royalty and freemasons. Rather than changing his theory, he chooses to dismiss her evidence.

Knight stated that the medical evidence showed that Kelly had been dead for five or six hours when her body was found at 10.45 a.m. Dr Phillips did declare that Kelly had been dead for five or six hours it is true, but he examined her body at 1.30 p.m. – not 10.45 a.m. The only person to see Mary Jane Kelly's body at 10.45 a.m. was Thomas Bowyer, who peeked through the window and discovered to his horror that Kelly was dead.

Against the '4 a.m. Scenario' is the evidence of Caroline Maxwell. Mrs Maxwell lived in the same street as Kelly and knew her by sight. She had chatted to her before and claimed to have spoken to her at about 8.30 a.m. on Friday, 9 November. Half an hour later, she saw Kelly talking to a 'short, dark man'. Less than two hours later, Kelly was discovered dead in her room.

We therefore have two different interpretations of what happened that night. In the '4 a.m. Scenario', George Hutchinson sees Mary Jane Kelly with her killer at 2 a.m. Kelly is murdered at about 4 a.m., managing to utter a cry of 'Murder!' Her killer then disembowels and mutilates her body and burns evidence in the fire before leaving at 6.15 a.m.

The alternative scenario, however, is that George Hutchinson saw Kelly with a client at 2 a.m. Since she was a prostitute, there was nothing sinister or unusual about her taking men back to her room. Her room was cold and she was forced to build up a good fire. It is not known when her client left, although it is possible that he left at 6.15 a.m. Kelly could not sleep and went out about two hours later. She met Caroline Maxwell and chatted to her. About 9 a.m., she met a short, dark man in the street. She took him into her room. He killed her almost immediately and then mutilated her body. It is not known at what time he left, although he had obviously made his escape by the time Thomas Bowyer discovered the body at 10.45 a.m.

If we are to accept the '4 a.m. Scenario' over the '9 a.m. Scenario', we have to discount the evidence of Caroline Maxwell. But how likely is it that Mrs Maxwell made a mistake? The inquest took place on Monday, 12 November, three days after the discovery of the body. People's memories can become confused over time but three days is not a long period: it is not long enough for someone with normal powers of recollection to become confused.

But we also need to think about life in 1888. There were no televisions and no radios, people did not live the socially isolated lives that we lead now. People took a lot more interest in what their neighbours were doing: sometimes, they would stand at their front doorsteps and watch the comings-and-goings in the street. Much more time was spent in conversation with neighbours; people generally knew about everything that was going on in their neighbourhoods.

Shops tended to be situated locally and, because there was no motorised transport, people lived much closer to their places of work. An area like Dorset Street/Miller's Court would have its corner shops and people would be able to do their day-to-day shopping locally. It is worth noting that not only did Mrs Maxwell live in Dorset Street but her husband worked there. She was talking to Kelly at 8.30 a.m. on Friday. It is unlikely that she would have had reason to leave the Dorset Street/Miller's Court area that morning.

The body was discovered at 10.45 a.m. Uniformed police officers were standing outside Kelly's room and peering in through the window from about 11 a.m. People who were in the street going to the shops would have noticed. The gossip would have whizzed around the neighbourhood and the locals would have known what was going on long before John McCarthy broke the door down with an axe. That means Mrs Maxwell spoke to Kelly at 8.45 a.m. and probably learned that she had been murdered not long after 11 a.m.

If the '4 a.m. Scenario' is to be accepted, Mrs Maxwell must have been mistaken in her evidence. That means she either lied or made a mistake about the date of her conversation with Kelly. She must have begun to believe that a conversation she had on the preceding Wednesday or Thursday had actually taken place on Friday. But is this likely?

Mrs Maxwell said she spoke to Kelly at 8.30 a.m. Within two and half hours, there are policemen hanging around outside Kelly's door and it is obvious to everyone in the street that something has happened. Is Mrs Maxwell likely to have made a mistake under those circumstances? Surely the dramatic news of the murder would have fixed her conversation with Kelly indelibly in her mind?

A few days later, it is reasonable to argue that she might have become confused over the date. But it is not credible to suggest that she became confused over the date of a conversation that took place two hours before the discovery of the body. Put simply, she could not have learned that Kelly had been murdered and then somehow start to believe that a conversation she had with Kelly two days earlier had actually taken place two hours earlier.

What, then, of the medical evidence? As Begg, Fido and Skinner have already shown in *The Jack the Ripper A–Z*, forensic science was in its infancy in 1888 and could not be expected to yield accurate results. Dr Phillips estimated that Kelly had been dead for five or six hours when he examined the body at 1.30 p.m. This gives the time of death as somewhere between 7.30 and 8.30 a.m. which does not support either the 9 a.m. or the 4 a.m. scenarios.

Doctors would estimate the times of death by taking the internal body temperature and then guessing the likely rate of cooling. Obviously, much depended on the skill and experience of the doctor. Moreover, a body which had been disembowelled would lose heat more quickly than one which had not. It is unlikely that Dr Phillips had much experience in guessing the times of death of bodies which had been disembowelled. His conclusions may be nothing more than guesswork or – if you'll forgive the pun – a stab in the dark.

If we are to discount the '9 a.m. Scenario', it means that Mrs Maxwell was either feeble-minded, had a bad memory or was a liar. But no evidence has ever been put forward to support any of these assertions.

What has happened with the murder of Mary Jane Kelly is that most writers and researchers have become so convinced that they are hunting for a Dr Jekyll-type character that they have discounted the evidence of the only witness who actually saw Kelly with her killer – because that evidence does not fit their pre-conceived ideas of what must have happened.

Mrs Maxwell said that she saw Kelly with a 'short dark man' at 9 a.m. on Friday. In all probability, that man was Jack the Ripper.

18

THE MODUS OPERANDI

SEVEN WOMEN WERE MURDERED IN WHITECHAPEL DURING 1888. It is agreed that five were murdered by a single assailant known by the name of 'Jack the Ripper'. The injuries they received were as follows:

- Polly Nichols – throat cut, abdomen cut open;
- Annie Chapman – breathing interfered with before death, throat cut and abdomen cut open;
- Elizabeth Stride – throat cut only;
- Catherine Eddowes – throat cut, abdomen cut open, face mutilated;
- Mary Jane Kelly – throat cut, abdomen cut open, face mutilated, breasts cut off, chest cut open.

It is generally accepted that the murderer strangled his victims prior to mutilation. Not only does it explain why no cries were heard from the victims but it is also consistent with the injuries they received. All the victims were found lying in such a way that their appearance gave the impression they had been fighting for their throats but it was only in the case of Chapman that the examining doctor was able to say so unequivocally.

In *The Jack the Ripper A–Z*, Begg, Fido and Skinner give the modus operandi of Jack the Ripper as follows: the killer stood in front of his victims in the normal position for standing intercourse but seized them by the throat with both hands, silencing them and inducing unconsciousness; he then let them fall onto their backs before cutting the throat and making other mutilations (except in the case of Stride).

Just to show how problematic these matters are, Donald Rumbelow suggested a different modus operandi in *The Complete Jack the Ripper*. His hypothesis was that the victims lifted their skirts and bent forwards to allow penetration from the rear and that the killer strangled them and then cut their throats from behind.

Nevertheless, a typical Ripper attack does have a style that can be agreed on: it may not be clear whether the attack came from the front or the rear but, in either case, we have death by strangulation followed by the cutting of the throat and the slashing open of the abdomen. But how does all this compare with the injuries received by Ellen Bury? It is the same in the sense that her killer attacked her in the same two places – the throat and the abdomen. The only difference is that, this time, the throat was not cut. In Ellen Bury's case, she was simply strangled and had her belly cut open.

The style of the attack on Ellen Bury is very similar to the style of the attack on both Nichols and Chapman. Arguments can be made to suggest that the attacks on Stride, Eddowes and Kelly also followed the same pattern. It is possible that Stride's abdomen would have been cut open if the killer had not been interrupted in his work. The cause of death of Eddowes was the same but, presumably, her killer felt he had time to mutilate her face before fleeing. And in Kelly's case, because he was in an enclosed room, he had more time to work without fear of interruption.

Ellen Bury's injuries are not identical with those of the other victims. However, she was killed by strangulation and her murderer then proceeded to mutilate her abdomen. The similarity is clear.

But there is a question we must ask ourselves: how significant is it that Ellen Bury's throat was not cut? There may be a very simple reason why William Bury did not cut her throat: he did not need to. Most of the Jack the Ripper murders were committed in the open street where it was important for the murderer to bring on death as quickly as possible without allowing the victim to cry out.

Jack the Ripper had to cut the throats of his victims after strangling them. After strangling them, he would not have been completely sure that he had killed them. After a woman has lost consciousness, how long do you keep up the pressure on her neck to cause death? And what if she has feigned the loss of consciousness in an attempt to save her life? By cutting the throat, the Ripper was simply making sure that the deed was done and that the woman could not waken up and cry out. The severing of the throat would have the added advantage of severing the vocal cords if it did not bring about death instantaneously.

The difference with the murder in Dundee is that the killer had more time. The murder was committed in the bedroom of a basement flat. There was no prospect of policemen on the beat or innocent bystanders walking by. No one was going to stumble across the murder scene by accident. The killer was under less pressure of time: he could take longer to strangle his victim because no one was going to interrupt him.

Consider the murder in Mitre Square which was executed during the 15-minute interval before PC Watkins's beat took him back into the square. The killer had to take his victim into the square, murder her silently and then disfigure the body before making his escape in the space of less than 15 minutes. Strangulation produced a silent death but it would be hard to tell the precise moment when the victim died because there would be a period of time when the victim had lost consciousness but was still alive. The cutting of the throat was a way of making sure.

But with William Bury kneeling over his victim in the full knowledge that there was no possibility of interruption, the cutting of the throat is less necessary. Suppose he had not killed his wife outright and that she had shown signs of regaining consciousness while his knife was at work in her abdomen? In that situation, William Bury would have had plenty of time to renew the pressure around her neck and to maintain it until she was dead.

Jack the Ripper had to cut the throats of his London victims. William Bury did not have to cut the throat of his known victim. And the fact that Ellen Bury's throat was not cut should not be regarded as evidence that her killer was *not* Jack the Ripper.

So now we come to the next question: do any of the descriptions given by witnesses of Jack the Ripper fit William Bury? Before we can answer this, we must decide which witnesses saw Jack the Ripper.

As far as we know, no one saw Polly Nichols in the company of her murderer. Elizabeth Long saw Annie Chapman talking to a man in Hanbury Street at 5.30 a.m., only minutes before her murder. So little time elapsed between Long's sighting of Chapman and her murder that it is safe to assume that the man Long saw was Jack the Ripper. Unfortunately, Long did not say very much other than that the man had dark hair, wore a deerstalker hat and spoke with a foreign accent. The man was only a little taller than Chapman, who was about 5 ft tall. William Bury had dark hair and was 5 ft 3½ in. tall. So the description Long gave does not eliminate Bury as a suspect.

The only thing that might eliminate Bury is the foreign accent – if we knew what it was. Bury would have had a Wolverhampton or Midlands accent, which, in the days before radio, might have been unfamiliar to Long. Hence, it might have sounded to her like a foreign accent. And Elizabeth Stride was seen with a man who wore a peaked cap. And Catherine Eddowes was seen with a man who wore a cloth cap with a peak.

PC William Smith made the statement that he saw a man of about 28 years of age talking to Elizabeth Stride. Why Smith said the man was about 28 years old rather than about 30 years of age, which would seem more normal, only he can tell. But William Bury was exactly 28 years old at this time. So Smith's statement does not eliminate Bury.

Caroline Maxwell said she saw Mary Jane Kelly in the company of a short, dark man shortly before her murder. As we have said, William Bury was 5 ft 3½ in. tall with dark hair. Again, the description does not eliminate him.

PC Smith also saw a man with Elizabeth Stride about half an hour before her murder. It is by no means certain that the man seen by PC Smith was the killer: there was plenty of time for him to leave Stride and for her to meet another possible client. It should be remembered that a prostitute working the streets might approach several men within the space of about a minute.

PC Smith described the man he saw as being 5 ft 7 in. tall. Being a police constable, it is likely that Smith was experienced in giving descriptions and was able to give one that was reasonably accurate. If he saw the killer, that would appear to exclude William Bury because the man Smith saw was four inches taller than Bury.

However, Smith's identification of a possible suspect as being 5 ft 7 in. tall is suspicious and throws up a lot of the difficulties with eyewitness accounts that are given after the event. When Smith saw the man, he did not know he was looking at a murder suspect. It was only later, when Elizabeth Stride was found dead, that Smith realised the man he saw might have been Jack the Ripper. But was he unconsciously guided into identifying the man he saw as being 5 ft 7 in. tall?

After the murder of Annie Chapman, the London Metropolitan Police issued the following description of a suspect on Tuesday 11 September, 1888: 'Age 37, height 5 ft 7 in., rather dark beard and moustache. Dress – shirt, dark jacket, dark vest and trousers, black scarf and black felt hat. Spoke with a foreign accent.'

On Saturday, 15 September 1888, it was reported in the newspapers that a man had been arrested in connection with the Whitechapel murders. He was 5 ft 7 in. or 5 ft 8 in. tall.

Then, on Tuesday, 18 September, the following report appeared in *The Times*:

> William Eade, a signalman in the employ of the East London Railway Company, saw a man on the line of the morning of Saturday 8th. Eade was coming down the Cambridge Heath road when he saw a man on the opposite side of the street. About 4 in. of a blade of a long knife was sticking out of the man's trouser pocket. Eade followed him. As soon as he saw he was being followed, the man quickened his pace. Eade lost sight of him under some railway arches. He was about 5 ft 8 in., 35 years of age, with dark moustache and whiskers. He wore a double peak cap, dark brown jacket and a pair of overalls above dark trousers.

The significance of the date (8 September) was that it was the same day as the murder of Annie Chapman. However, the man chased by Eade was identified later as one Henry James, whom *The Times* called a 'well-known harmless lunatic'. By then, though, the damage had been done: the public had already been told, more than once, that the police were looking for someone about 5 ft 7 in. or 5 ft 8 in. tall.

When people like PC Smith were thinking back to the previous day's events, having learned that they may have set eyes upon the killer, it is possible that they allowed themselves to be unconsciously influenced. If they thought the Ripper was 5 ft 7 in. tall then maybe they assumed that the man they saw was about that height.

However, it should also be remembered that PC Smith's evidence is not crucial. The man he saw was with Stride a whole half hour before she was murdered. There was plenty of time for Stride to have parted company with that man and then to have met another man – especially as she was known to be a prostitute who worked the streets.

What this means is that we have to be careful when selecting witness descriptions of Jack the Ripper. It may sound like an obvious thing to say but we have to be sure that the person the witness saw was actually Jack the Ripper. Therefore, we are looking for sightings very close to the time of death. Needless to say, there are very few.

Elizabeth Long saw a man with Annie Chapman at 5.30 a.m. The murder was committed at 5.32 a.m. The man Long saw was almost certainly the killer.

James Brown saw a man with Elizabeth Stride about 15 minutes before her murder. It seems probable that the man Brown saw was the killer.

Catherine Eddowes was seen with a man wearing a peaked cap at 1.35 a.m. Her dead body was found by PC Watkins at 1.45 a.m., making it highly probable that the man seen with her was the killer.

It is intriguing that a man wearing a peaked cap was seen with Elizabeth Stride one hour before her murder. Was this the same man who was seen with Eddowes ten minutes before her murder? It might be but this hypothesis is not supported by the evidence of James Brown. Brown said the man he saw was wearing a long, black coat but Brown made no mention of a cap. However, it needs to be borne in mind that Brown glanced at the rear of the man: in the darkness and in a badly lit street, he may not have noticed a peaked cap – especially as the peak would have been pulled forward over the face.

Finally, Caroline Maxwell may have seen Mary Jane Kelly's killer. But Mrs Maxwell saw someone with Kelly at 9 a.m. and there was time for that person to have left and for another man to have entered Kelly's room before the discovery of the body at

10.45 a.m. We will assume that she got a glimpse of the killer, even though this is a probability, not a certainty.

If we accept the descriptions given by these witnesses, what are we left with? Jack the Ripper was a small, dark-haired man who wore a long, black coat and a peaked cap. He had a foreign accent, although by 'foreign' we may simply mean that he was not local to the East End of London.

And that is all we have.

19

BURKE, HARE AND JACK THE RIPPER

DID JACK THE RIPPER HAVE SURGICAL SKILL? THIS NEEDS TO BE looked at because, if he did, that would eliminate William Bury. Bury's father was a fishmonger but there is absolutely no evidence that Bury was trained in the art of gutting fish. And even if he was, we still cannot say he had any surgical skill.

Surgical skill on the part of Jack the Ripper is, to paraphrase Dugald McKechnie, a central plank of some of the more grandiloquent theories. This concept very much follows the 'Dr Jekyll' line of thought. Because the idea that the Ripper might have had some surgical skill is a popular one and because it clearly excludes William Bury, it is important that we spend some time looking at it.

The first person to promote the theory that Jack the Ripper had surgical knowledge was Coroner Wynne Baxter, who made the following statement at the inquest into the death of Annie Chapman:

> There were two things missing. Her rings had been wrenched from her fingers and had not since been found, and the uterus had been taken from the abdomen. The body had not been dissected but the injuries had been made by someone who had considerable anatomical skill and knowledge. There were no meaningless cuts. The organ had been taken by one who knew where to find it . . . No unskilled person could have known where to find it or have recognised it when it was found.

There are two flaws in Baxter's logic but, to be fair, he was working in very difficult circumstances. Not only was Forensic Science in its infancy but Chapman's body had actually been stripped and washed before it could be examined.

Baxter assumed that there were no meaningless cuts because he believed that death had been caused by the cutting of the throat. But if the victim's throat had been cut while her heart was still pumping, blood would have sprayed out in all directions and she would still have been able to scream. The absence of blood at the murder scene and the silence with which the murder was committed both pointed to strangulation being the cause of death. And if strangulation was the cause of death, then the cutting of the throat afterwards must be regarded as a meaningless cut. The poor conditions under which Baxter worked drew him towards a faulty conclusion.

Whoever killed Chapman removed her uterus. The missing organ was never found by the police. It is obvious that it would take surgical skill and anatomical knowledge to remove a uterus from a corpse. But this line of thought assumes that the killer intended to remove the uterus. Coroner Baxter did not take account of the possibility that the killer may have opened Chapman's abdomen and cut something out without having any idea what it was.

It needs to be remembered that Chapman was the second victim and that the police did not know, at this point, that they were looking for a serial killer. Here, again, Coroner Baxter may have been led up a blind alley because he was looking for a motive for a motiveless killing.

We now know that the Whitechapel murders were a series of sexually motivated murders by a serial killer going under the name of Jack the Ripper. But Coroner Baxter did not know that when he conducted the inquest into the murder of Annie Chapman. He was investigating a single murder which he did not connect to any other murders. The possibility that this was part of a sexually motivated serial killing was not considered.

In looking for a motive, Coroner Baxter seemed drawn towards the shocking crimes of Burke and Hare which had occurred in Edinburgh 60 years previously. Because the medical students at Edinburgh University needed a constant supply of human bodies for dissection and study, William Burke and William Hare started up the lucrative business of murdering people and selling their bodies to Dr Knox at the university.

In looking for a motive, Baxter focused his attention on the missing uterus with the idea that English equivalents of Burke and Hare had gone into business. This may have led Baxter to the assumption that the killer was a surgeon or lecturer in anatomy and therefore must have had some surgical skill. The Coroner's very logical, but misguided, thinking on the matter was published in *The Times*:

> The conclusion that the desire was to possess the missing abdominal organ seemed overwhelming. If the object were robbery, the injuries to the viscera were meaningless, for death had previously resulted from the loss of blood at the neck. Moreover, when they found an easily accomplished theft of some paltry brass rings and an internal organ taken, after at least a quarter of an hour's work and by a skilled person, they were driven to the deduction that the abstraction of the missing portion of the abdominal viscera was the object, and the theft of the rings was a thin-veiled blind, an attempt to prevent the real intention being discovered. The amount missing would go into a breakfast cup, and had not the medical examination been of a thorough and searching character, it might easily have been left unnoticed that there was any portion of the body which had been taken. The difficulty in believing the purport of the murderer was the possession of the missing abdominal organ was natural. It was abhorrent to their feelings to conclude that a life should be taken for so slight an object; but when rightly considered the reasons for most murders were altogether out of all proportion to their guilt. It had been suggested that the criminal was a lunatic with morbid feelings. That might or might not be the case, but the object of the murderer appeared palpably shown by the facts, and it was not necessary to assume lunacy, for it was clear there was a market for the missing organ.

This Burke-and-Hare analysis followed the deduction that the possession of the uterus was the motive for the murder. This analysis seemed to be supported by the murder of Catherine

Eddowes, whose kidney was removed by the killer. At the Eddowes inquest, under questioning by the solicitor, Dr Gordon Brown testified that the killer did have some surgical knowledge:

> MR CRAWFORD: Would you consider that the person who inflicted the wounds possessed great anatomical skill?
>
> DR BROWN: A good deal of knowledge as to the position of the organs in the abdominal cavity and the way of removing them.
>
> MR CRAWFORD: You spoke of abstraction of the left kidney. Would it require great skill and knowledge to remove it?
>
> DR BROWN: It would require a great deal of knowledge as to its position to remove it. It is easily overlooked. It is covered by membrane.

Dr Brown appeared to be giving a very definite answer. However, he was later to contradict himself.

> MR CRAWFORD: Would not such knowledge be likely to be possessed by one accustomed to cutting up animals?
>
> DR BROWN: Yes.

Brown's Burke-and-Hare analysis assumes that the killer intended to remove the kidney. This was the same kind of thinking that led Coroner Baxter towards the flawed assumption that there were no meaningless cuts.

It may have seemed to Baxter that, in the case of Chapman, there were no meaningless cuts – if the murder was committed by a medical student who needed to dissect a uterus. But, in other murders, there did appear to be meaningless cuts. Consider the following statement about Catherine Eddowes's injuries:

> The liver was stabbed as if by the point of a sharp knife. There was another incision in the liver, about 2½ in., and, below, the left lobe of the liver was slit through by a vertical cut . . . There was a stab of about an inch in the left groin, penetrating the skin in superficial fashion. Below that was a cut of 3 in., going through all the tissues, wounding the peritoneum to about the same extent.

These wounds strongly suggest that the killer was cutting and slashing Eddowes's body at random.

Two other doctors also gave evidence at the Eddowes inquest. They were doctors George Sequeira and William Saunders. The City Solicitor also asked them if, in their opinions, the killer had any surgical skill. Dr Sequeira was first to testify.

> MR CRAWFORD: Judging from the injuries inflicted, do you
>   think he was possessed of great surgical skill?
> DR SEQUEIRA: No, I do not.

At the Eddowes inquest, therefore, two doctors were of the opinion that the killer had no surgical skill while one (Brown) thought he had the skill not of a surgeon but of someone who worked in an abattoir.

In 1888, the theory that the killer either worked in an abattoir or had some kind of contact with animals was mooted more strongly than the idea that he was a surgeon. The surgeon theory grew as the 'Dr Jekyll' impression of the killer grew. But unlike the theory that the killer was a surgeon, the theory that he worked with animals had some logic behind it. This theory was based on the curious fact that Jack the Ripper only seemed to strike at weekends. The five dates of the Ripper murders do seem to suggest that the killer was working to some kind of pattern: Nichols was killed on a Friday, Chapman on a Saturday, Stride and Eddowes on a Sunday and Kelly on a Friday.

Cattle boats were in the habit of coming into the Thames on Thursdays or Fridays and leaving again on Sundays or Mondays. It seemed possible to some that the murderer was a drover or butcher employed on one of these boats, of which there were many, and that he periodically appeared and disappeared with one of the steamers. *The Times* turned its attention to this theory after the murder of Mary Jane Kelly, as the following quotation shows:

> When the former murders were under discussion, it was
> noted as a curious fact that they occurred about the end of
> the week, and this and other circumstances suggested the
> theory that the assassin did not habitually live in London,
> but visited it at intervals – that he came, to state one form
> of this theory, in one of the cattle boats which weekly call

here. Some circumstances attending this latest crime give more plausibility to this suggestion. But whoever he may be, it is plain that some wild beast in human shape haunts the resorts of the outcasts of the East End to lure them to a terrible death.

It is a mystery to this author why this reasonable and plausible theory was never investigated by the police.

20

THE HANGMAN

THERE WAS ONE MAN WHO BELIEVED HE CAME FACE TO FACE with Jack the Ripper in April 1889. This was a man who had killed far more people than the notorious Whitechapel Murderer. When the two men met, Jack the Ripper had accounted for five or six women. The other man had been responsible for 67 deaths and would go on to kill more than 100. If you asked him, he would have said that some of them had deserved it and others had not. His name was James Berry and he was the public hangman.

James Berry was 37 years old in 1889. This former Bradford policeman had tried his luck as a shoe salesman before he became the public hangman in 1884. The previous hangman, William Marwood, had died and Berry successfully applied for the vacancy. Marwood was the inventor of the long drop and the man who transformed the image of hanging. For more than 1,000 years previously, condemned men and women had slowly strangled on the end of the rope. Marwood invented the long drop to snap the neck. Instead of a barbaric mediaeval practice in which the condemned would wriggle about on the end of the rope as he gasped for breath while crowds watched in fascination, hanging became a skilled job in which the condemned was dispatched quickly and painlessly.

The practice of hanging had given the English language the phrase, 'You're pulling my leg!' When a condemned man was hanged, his friends and relatives would pull on his legs. This would increase the pressure on his neck and hasten his death.

Thus, if you're pulling someone's leg, you're putting them out of their misery.

But the concept of hanging as a swift and merciful method of execution was less than ten years old when James Berry became the public hangman. Only Marwood had used the long drop before him. But although Marwood left notes and a set of tables so that the length of drop based on the weight of the condemned could be calculated, he did not train any apprentices.

Marwood had found that the knot should be placed below the condemned man's left ear to jerk the head backwards and break the neck. If it was placed on the right side of the neck, the rope would jerk the head forwards and result in death by strangulation. The length of the drop was calculated to produce a blow equivalent to 1,260 pounds. When this figure was divided by the weight of the prisoner in pounds, the result was the length of the drop in feet. For example, a prisoner weighing 168 lb would be given a drop of seven and a half feet. However, these were general guidelines which took no account of things like the build or age of the prisoner or the wear and tear on the neck. For example, would an 80-year-old man with thin skin and wasted muscles require the same length of drop as a fit and healthy 20-year-old?

James Berry had never worked with Marwood and some of his executions went badly wrong. Sometimes, he calculated too long a drop and decapitated the prisoner. Sometimes, he calculated too short a drop and did not kill the prisoner outright but was forced to wait for him to expire on the end of the rope as in the old days. Sometimes doctors, not trusting Berry, would intervene and make him use a longer drop resulting in decapitation for the prisoner.

Nevertheless, the invention of the long drop allowed the authorities to present hanging as a humanitarian method of execution in which the condemned was dispatched into oblivion within a fraction of a second – the length of time it took him to fall the six or seven feet that the hangman had calculated.

The length of the drop was calculated to break the neck without decapitating the body. Decapitation was not seen as a sacking offence by the authorities; it was merely undesirable. If the hangman misjudged the weights and gave the condemned too long a drop, the force of the falling body might snap the head off the moment the rope was pulled tight. This resulted in a mess; the pit underneath the trapdoor would be full of blood and the ghastly spectacle in front of magistrates, press and public did nothing to restore hanging's image as a clean and quick method of execution. However, it was generally agreed that decapitation was preferable to slow suffocation and, consequently, hangmen who decapitated their prisoners were not punished.

The idea, however, was for the hangman to execute an efficient death in which the condemned died instantaneously and in which no damage was done to the body beyond the breaking of the neck. This necessitated good judgement about the length of the drop. Although Marwood's tables set out his calculations there was, in truth, no substitute for the experience and skill of the executioner.

What this meant was that James Berry was certain to have spent some time in William Bury's cell, measuring his height and weight. Whatever conversation passed between the two men was unrecorded at the time but there are apocryphal stories. An article by R. Storrier in *The Tayside Police Magazine* recounts the story that James Berry questioned the condemned man about his involvement in the Whitechapel murders. William Bury is supposed to have replied, 'I suppose you think you are clever because you are going to hang me – but you are not going to get anything out of me.' However, a contemporary source for the story cannot be traced, so we cannot say whether it is true or untrue.

James Berry resigned as public hangman in 1892, aged 40. He lived on for another 21 years, during which time he became something of an embarrassment to the Home Office because he suffered from alcohol addiction and – amazingly – toured the country preaching for the abolition of the death penalty.

Berry wrote a book about his life entitled *My Experiences as an Executioner*, in which no mention of William Bury or Jack the Ripper was made. During this 21-year period, however, this unstable former executioner was someone who could be plied with drink by those who wanted to tease questions out of him.

One man who did so was a journalist in Newmarket called Ernest A. Parr. On 28 March 1908 he wrote to the Secretary of State for Scotland:

Sir

I have for some time past been gathering matter bearing upon the subject of the 'Jack the Ripper' murders and today came across the statement in a paper that a man named William Henry Bury, who was charged at Dundee Circuit Court on March 28th, 1889, with wife murder, acknowledged that he was the 'Ripper' and after sentence of death was passed on him for the murder of his wife, Bury 'made a full confession of the Ripper crimes, which document was forwarded to the Secretary for Scotland.' In the course of my inquiries I have several times come across details which appear to point to this man as having committed the crimes and during a conversation with Berry the ex-Public Executioner, that individual told me explicitly that Bury was known to have been Jack the Ripper . . .

Ernest A. Parr

This statement from Ernest Parr could hardly have been more definite, although Parr did not give the time and place of his meeting with Berry. Berry was still alive in 1908. The murders were only 20 years old.

21

THE EVIDENCE AGAINST WILLIAM BURY

WHAT, THEN, DO WE KNOW ABOUT JACK THE RIPPER? ONLY THAT he was a short, dark-haired man who was not a Londoner. The description we have does not allow us to eliminate William Bury.

But what is the evidence against William Bury? The biggest single piece of evidence is that his modus operandi – death by strangulation followed by mutilation of the abdomen – was strikingly similar to Jack the Ripper's. Judging from the injuries to Mrs Bury, the Ripper victims suffered injuries consistent with what we might expect if William Bury was responsible.

There was one other similarity. Only two of these women were murdered indoors – Mary Jane Kelly and Ellen Bury. In both cases, each woman was wearing only a chemise at the time of the discovery of the body.

Jack the Ripper was able to walk the streets at all times of the day. Nichols, Stride and Eddowes were all killed in darkness during the early hours of the morning but Chapman was definitely killed during the daylight, and Kelly seems to have been killed in daylight, although many researchers have chosen not to believe it.

After the murder of Chapman, the killer fled through the streets with blood on his clothes with the time approaching 6 a.m. This is very important because a lot of shift workers worked from 6 a.m. till 6 p.m. The killer was obviously somebody who did not have to be at his work by 6 a.m. The same applies to the murder of Kelly: whoever killed her was wandering along Dorset Street at 9 a.m. This eliminates everybody who would have been noticed missing from their place of work at those times.

But William Bury cannot be eliminated. He was a self-employed sawdust merchant, able to work – or not to work – his own hours. Most of the time, as we know, he preferred to live off his wife's inheritance. He therefore had the time to commit these crimes and could be wandering about the streets when other people had to be at work.

William Bury did not return home every night. James Martin gave evidence at his trial that Ellen Bury would sometimes go out looking for her husband because he had been absent from home for two or three days. One scenario we have is that Jack the Ripper probably did not go home on the nights of the murders but was, instead, lying low in a common lodging house till the commotion died down. Again, Bury cannot be eliminated.

Mrs Elizabeth Haynes also testified that she saw Bury kneeling on top of his wife brandishing a table knife and apparently about to cut her throat. He only desisted when Haynes threatened to fetch a policeman. The only difference between Bury's crime and the crimes of Jack the Ripper is that he did not cut his victim's throat in Dundee. But he seems to have attempted exactly that in Swaton Road, Bow, on 7 April 1888.

We can therefore make the following statements without fear of contradiction:

- William Bury was capable of committing crimes like the Whitechapel murders;
- he had the opportunity to do so;
- the Whitechapel murders began after he arrived in London;
- the murders ceased when he left London.

We can also say that William Bury's actions were consistent with a psychopathic pattern of behaviour. This is indicated by his dramatic change of character: from being a violent and aggressive man, he turned into a quiet and considerate husband while he plotted his wife's murder. He also stole from his wife, assaulted her, frightened her by sleeping with a knife under his pillow, gave her a venereal disease, reduced her to a life of utter misery . . . yet showed absolutely no guilt or remorse. This complete lack of any conscience is consistent with the psychopathic personality.

The graffiti *Jack Ripper is at the back of this door* and *Jack Ripper is in this seller* was found written in chalk on a door and a wall of Bury's basement flat in Dundee. According to the *Dundee Advertiser*, the writing was made before Ellen Bury's body was discovered. That means it could not have been written by a member of the public after the body was found but could only have been written by an occupant of the house before the body was found. No guests were ever invited into the house while the Burys lived there, meaning that the writing had to have made by either William or Ellen Bury.

Finally, Lieutenant James Parr of Dundee Police stated that William Bury said he was afraid he would be arrested as Jack the Ripper.

If we put it all together, the picture we have built up looks like the following. William Bury moved to London in the autumn of 1887. One year later, a shocking series of murders were committed in the capital. William Bury moved to Dundee in January 1889, and there were no more murders in London. But there was a murder in Dundee in February 1889, in which the killer uses a very similar modus operandi to that of Jack the Ripper. He may have attempted to confess to the Jack the Ripper murders whilst in the custody of Dundee Police but we cannot say for sure because his exact words were not written down. However, a confession of sorts was written in chalk on the wall and on the back of a door in his basement flat in Princes Street, Dundee. Bearing in mind that the writing was made before the discovery of the body and that no one entered Bury's apartment during the two weeks he lived there, there is only one possible author of these chalk marks: William Bury himself. James Berry, the man who hanged William Bury, is reported to have said that it was 'known' that William Bury was the Ripper.

To summarise, let us say the following: William Bury was a murderer who used the same modus operandi as Jack the Ripper. He arrived in London before the Whitechapel murders began and left after they had finished. He committed a Ripper-style murder in Dundee. He left an oblique confession written in chalk on the wall of his basement flat. The two Dundee newspapers, the *Advertiser* and the *Courier*, suspected him of involvement in the Whitechapel murders, and the public hangman, James Berry, believed that William Bury and Jack the Ripper was one and the same man.

EPILOGUE

IMAGINE THAT WILLIAM BURY WENT ON TRIAL IN LONDON charged with the Whitechapel murders. If I had been leading the Prosecution and was charged with the task of delivering a summing-up to the jury, this is what I would say:

> Ladies and Gentlemen of the jury, the man standing before you is a man without a conscience. He has shown no remorse either for the murder of his wife or for his shocking treatment of her while she was alive. He is a man who is incapable of feeling sympathy for his fellow human beings.
>
> If we were told that Jack the Ripper had come north to Dundee and committed a murder, then I put it to you that the murder of Ellen Bury is exactly the type of murder that we would expect to see. Not content with murdering his victim, William Bury mutilated her corpse very much in the same manner as Jack the Ripper. Like Jack the Ripper, he was a man who liked getting his knife into the abdomen of his victim.
>
> Like Jack the Ripper, William Bury was a short, dark-haired man. He left London after the murder of Mary Jane Kelly, which explains the sudden cessation of the Ripper murders. Ladies and Gentlemen, there is no Jack the Ripper mystery. There is only the appearance of a mystery because the perpetrator of these murders moved from one city to another. Those who wish to look for Jack the Ripper in London will look in vain because he moved out of that city on 19 January 1889. And those who wish to believe that he was an eminent

member of London society are simply not looking at the evidence.

William Bury was a psychopath who is known to have been living in the East End of London at the time of the Ripper murders. And it is surely significant that there were no more Ripper murders in London since William Bury left the city in January 1889.

We know that William Bury went missing from home for two or three days at a time when he was living in London. We do not know what he was doing but we know that he had the ability to disappear and that he had somewhere to go on the nights when he did not go home. On the nights when Jack the Ripper was covered in blood, he could not have gone home and must have had somewhere else to go.

We know that William Bury was wandering the streets in the small hours – the time of Annie Chapman's murder. We know also that he was a self-employed sawdust merchant who did not have to report to work at 6 a.m. (or any other time). He therefore had the time to wander the streets in the mornings, looking for victims.

William Bury may have attempted to confess to the Ripper murders while in the custody of Dundee Police but the policeman on duty – Lieutenant James Parr – did not write his remarks down at the time. However, there can be no doubt that Bury also left a confession written in chalk on the walls of the flat he occupied in Dundee.

The similarities between the crime William Bury committed in Dundee and the crimes of Jack the Ripper are obvious, but the most damning piece of evidence is surely that of James Berry, the public hangman. What passed between Berry and William Bury on the eve of the execution is something we will never know but we do know that Berry explicitly stated that William Bury was known to have been Jack the Ripper.

Ladies and Gentlemen of the jury, I do not ask you to take my word for it. Take James Berry's words; take the words of William Bury himself. Consider the similarities between the murder in Princes Street, Dundee, and the crimes in Whitechapel. When you have considered all the evidence, I believe you will be led towards the inescapable conclusion that it was William Bury who committed the Whitechapel murders.